JUDSON PRESS
PUBLISHERS SINCE 1824

WHAT WE LOVE ABOUT THE BLACK CHURCH

CAN WE GET A WITNESS?

WILLIAM H. CROUCH JR.
AND JOEL C. GREGORY

Foreword by J. Alfred Smith Sr.
Afterword by Rhoda McKinney-Jones

JUDSON PRESS
PUBLISHERS SINCE 1824
VALLEY FORGE, PA

Interior design by Beth Oberholtzer.
Cover design by Tobias Becker, Birdbox Graphic Design,
www.birdboxdesign.com

Library of Congress Cataloging-in-Publication Data
Crouch, William H.
    What we love about the Black church : can we get a witness? / William H. Crouch, Jr. and Joel C. Gregory ; foreword by J. Alfred Smith, Sr. ; afterword by Rhoda McKinney-Jones. — 1st ed.
        p.   cm.
    Includes bibliographical references and index.
    ISBN 978-0-8170-1644-9 (pbk. : alk. paper) 1. African American churches. 2. African Americans—Religion. I. Gregory, Joel C., 1948– II. Title.

BR563.N4C76   2010
277.3'08308996073—dc22

                                                    2010010541

Printed on recycled paper in the U.S.A.
First Edition, 2010.

CONTENTS

Foreword by J. Alfred Smith Sr.   ix

Preface   xiii

Acknowledgments   xix

1. PREACHING   1
   With responses from Al B. Sutton Jr. and Cynthia L. Hale

2. ENCOURAGEMENT   11
   With responses from Maurice Watson and
   Jewel M. London

3. LAUGHTER AND LIGHT   21
   With responses from Denny D. Davis and
   Pamela R. Rivera

4. MENTORING MINISTERS: THE NEXT
   GENERATION   29
   With responses from Donald Hilliard Jr., Jini Kilgore,
   and Bryan L. Carter

5. FREEDOM OF EXPRESSION   43
   With responses from Jacqueline A. Thompson and
   A. Louis Patterson Jr.

6. STURDY BRIDGES: HONORING ELDERS   51
   With responses from Susan K. Williams Smith and
   Ivan Douglas Hicks

7. THE POWER OF TOUCH   65
*With responses from Ralph Douglas West Sr. and
Leslie J. Bowling-Dyer*

8. THE FIRST LADY OF THE CHURCH   75
*With responses from John K. Jenkins Sr. and
Sheila M. Bailey*

9. HOSPITALITY   85
*With responses from Major Lewis Jemison and
Wanda Bolton-Davis*

10. GRATITUDE   93
*With responses from Melvin V. Wade Sr. and
Barbara J. Bowman*

11. EMPOWERMENT   101
*With responses from Gina M. Stewart, Joseph Evans,
and Bernestine Smith*

12. PRAISE AND RESPECT   115
*With responses from Valerie Miles-Tribble and
Stephen J. Thurston Sr.*

Afterword by Rhoda McKinney-Jones   125
About the Contributors   129

FOREWORD

The late Rev. Dr. E. K. Bailey, an author and peerless biblical expositor, and his friend Rev. Dr. Warren W. Wiersbe, who is renowned as a preacher-scholar, released a delightful book in March 2003 called *Preaching in Black and White*.[1] Both of these men, the first black and the second white, helped us to see how God has richly blessed two distinct and valuable preaching traditions.

In this new book, Dr. Joel Gregory and Dr. William Crouch Jr. take us to new and essential levels by discussing the practical aspects of black-church congregational life, from their observations and preaching experiences in black churches and with black pastors coast to coast. Their perspective as white clergy is not meant to denigrate the practices of white congregations or to elevate black congregations above the level of criticism. They are simply sharing how the black church has helped to shape their teachings, their ministries, and their interactions with God's people.

Drs. Gregory and Crouch preach and serve in a bicultural Christian community, a world where very few white pastors preach and serve. White pastors who are a part of the dominant culture have fewer experiences preaching in black churches and have few opportunities to engage black preachers in serious discussions about preaching styles, faith traditions, and congregational life. It is as if black culture is a subculture with minority status in the traditional white culture. And the black church experience is one of which the majority culture has little knowledge or understanding.

Drs. Gregory and Crouch are ambassadors of reconciliation for building bridges of communication that cross cultural chasms within the body of Christ. We all have been scarred by our struggles and have been deprived by living on our own islands of cultural isolation. God appears to be using these two pastors as "bridge-people," both to promote healing in the body of Christ and to inspire the church to present a unified witness of the healing power of Jesus Christ in a broken world.

Drs. Gregory and Crouch are learning what black preachers have been required to learn, and that is to be bicultural in America. But Crouch and Gregory are saying something more—that there are values in the life of the black church that are invisible to the white church, and those qualities need to be shared and celebrated. Just as the white church has much to offer the world, the black church also upholds values white pastors can use to enrich the life and ministry of their congregations.

For the sake of survival, African American pastors have had no choice but to learn the folkways and mores of the dominant culture while speaking to the particularity of their own people in a church that was born in slavery. In *The Heart of Black Preaching*, Rev. Dr. Cleophus J. LaRue reminds us that, "at its core the black sermon is not about what blacks have had to endure in America or their peculiar place as a people of color in this country. It is the sovereign God at work in and through those experiences that characterize the essence of powerful black preaching."[2] Drs. Gregory and Crouch understand that the effects of this preaching evoke powerful insights worthy enough to be shared with white clergy and laity.

In this magnificent work, Drs. Gregory and Crouch are bicultural people in the sense that they may be described as being "comfortable and at peace with black church styles or norms, while at the same time they do not abandon their own whiteness. They can appreciate cultural differences without the surrender of their identity in their own primary culture."[3]

In *The Souls of Black Folk,* W. E. B. Du Bois speaks of the preservation of the primary culture identity:

> He [the Negro] would not Africanize America, for America has too much to teach the world and Africa. He would not bleach his Negro soul in a flood of white Americanism, for he knows that Negro blood has a message for the world. He simply wishes to make it possible for a man to be both a Negro and an American, without being cursed and spit upon by his fellows, without having the doors of Opportunity closed roughly in his face. This, then, is the end of his striving: to be a co-worker in the kingdom of culture, to escape both death and isolation, to husband and use his best powers and his latent genius.[4]

As I read critically and reflect prayerfully on the musings of Drs. Gregory and Crouch, I cannot help but see the presence of Jesus Christ, our Reconciler, birthing a reversal of history. Instead of a new Martin Luther King Jr., who reached out to white clergy from the black-church side, Drs. Gregory and Crouch, as sons of the white church, reach out to their white peers with a book that offers blessings in blackness.

Let us, with unity in our diversity, use this book for the glory of God and a world that needs the healing of Jesus Christ, who transforms all cultures with the lordship of his presence.

J. Alfred Smith Sr.
Pastor Emeritus, Allen Temple Baptist Church
Distinguished Professor of Preaching and Church Ministries
American Baptist Seminary of the West
The Graduate Theological Union

NOTES

1. E. K. Bailey and Warren W. Wiersbe, *Preaching in Black and White* (Grand Rapids: Zondervan, 2003).

2. Cleophus J. LaRue, *The Heart of Black Preaching* (Louisville: John Knox Press, 1999), 115.

3. Marvin K. Mayers, *Christianity Confronts Culture: A Strategy for Cross-cultural Evangelism* (Grand Rapids: Zondervan, 1974), 243.

4. W. E. B. Du Bois, *The Souls of Black Folk* (New York: Random House, 2003), 6.

PREFACE

The unprecedented revival of a historic black college on a white college campus, an international movement teaching homiletics to working pastors, and the immersion of two white ministers into the black church happened as a stroke of Providence on a moonlit ride across Kentucky horse farms.

The heaviest weights sometimes hang by the thinnest wires. Dr. Eric Fruge, director of The Marshall Center for Christian Ministry, had attended Gambrell Street Baptist Church in Fort Worth, Texas, while Joel was the pastor in the late 1970s and early 1980s. They had had no contact for twenty years. Bill invited Dr. Fruge to join Georgetown College as capital campaign director in 2001. Dr. Fruge later asked Joel to teach a homiletics seminar to Georgetown pastoral alumni in September 2004. That led to an invitation to return to the college and a subsequent meeting with Bill in April 2005. The two of us first met that April on the Georgetown campus: Joel spoke at the annual pastors' conference, and Bill attended as president of Georgetown.

At the end of that particular stay, Bill took Joel to the Lexington, Kentucky, airport in the predawn dark. Joel was surprised a college president would awaken in the middle of the night to usher him to an early flight. As they drove, the white fences of the thoroughbred horse farms reflected moonlight on the Kentucky bluegrass, and a destiny-laden conversation took place.

Bill was intrigued with Joel's involvement in the black church. As a child in the 1950s, Bill had been saddened by watching his father, a noted pastor, coping with the ugliness of racism in Jackson, Mississippi. Bill had vowed as a child to do something about discrimination, if he ever had the power and position to do so. Bill also had a vision to diversify Georgetown College, which was located in the midst of the fifteen whitest counties in Kentucky. The vision he had for his school, a predominantly white college founded in 1787, was that it was to become a campus of diversity. That was some kind of vision.

Joel had some similar interests. The late Rev. Dr. E. K. Bailey had acted in grace to aid in renewing Joel's ministry after a difficult passage in Joel's life. Dr. Bailey had invited Joel to preach at his International Expository Preaching Conference, an act that was actually an endorsement of Joel's ministry. From that experience, Joel, a white, southern preacher, began to be invited to hundreds of black churches and conferences, and that, for the most part, was unprecedented. Joel wanted to create enduring ways to commemorate the ministry of the late Dr. Bailey, who was an innovative leader. Joel also wanted to lead diverse, small-group seminars on preaching that were certified by an accredited educational institution.

So, that is the story of how this journey began. Bill had a legacy dream from his childhood and a vision to diversify his college. Joel wanted to memorialize Dr. Bailey and find a way to conduct preaching seminars with a certifying academic partner. Neither could have imagined what would develop from those dreams and an early-morning car ride on the dark side of dawn.

Five years later, Bill has led a diversity effort at Georgetown College with stunning results. The percentage of students of color at the college had increased from 3 percent in 2005 to 10 percent by the fall of 2009. The college has set a goal of 20 percent by 2015. The dream to remember Dr. Bailey has morphed from naming a room after him at Georgetown College to a full-blown project to renew the spirit of his alma mater, Bishop College, a historic black college that closed in Dallas, Texas, in 1988. The Bishop College Alive project is designed to keep the spirit of Bishop College through a Bishop College Legacy Scholarship program, the creation of the Bishop College Heritage Homiletics, the establishment of the Bishop College Hall of Fame, and the celebration of annual homecomings.

That dream now has national support and represents the first time in American educational history that a predominantly white college has honored the alumni of a historically black college. Bill plans to build the Bishop College Center for Educational Excellence to perpetuate the spirit of Bishop College on his school's campus. Beyond that, Bill has spoken about his diversity efforts at the United Nations and to the Disney Corporation.

Joel's dream of leading accredited preaching seminars has come to fruition in the form of Proclaimers Place, a nationally recognized, continuing-education event for working preachers. Joel has led forty-four Proclaimers Place Seminars in eleven states and, significantly, at Regent's Park College of Oxford University, which has hosted nine of Joel's seminars over the course of five years, with a combined attendance of 160. This is believed to be the largest predominantly African American group to do an educational event in the history of the college. Participants have published three books of sermons based on the experience.

All of this began with a ride in the dark to the airport. Late in his career, Carl Jung wrote of synchronicity, that coming together of random events that appear to have nothing in common but are in fact profoundly related.[1] We have touched one another in a surprising constellation of events that have unfolded over decades. The destiny of a college almost as old as the United States has changed profoundly; Proclaimers Place continues to teach hundreds of preachers; a beloved black institution, Bishop College, has a new incarnation. And 160 black brothers and sisters have walked the venerable streets of Oxford. Who would have imagined?

And along the way, we experienced a growing conviction. The black church has a great deal to offer white churches. For much of America's religious history, whites have taken a patronizing attitude that they have a corner on the "right stuff" and need to help black churches with money, programs, and organization. Our journey has led us to another conclusion: black churches have strengths that would greatly enrich white churches. Hence this book, which celebrates some of those qualities.

Most books need some disclaimers, and here is ours. This book is not a research piece. It is the simple testimony of two white men of God and our experiences with the black church. One should look elsewhere for empirical or scientific conclusions. Neither is the book a blanket commendation of everything in the black church, no more than it is a wholesale condemnation of everything in the white church. Each church culture can learn from the other. One cannot appreciate another culture by disowning or demonizing one's own. We simply write as two seasoned ministers who affirm our own personal histories in the white church, yet we have become more fully human and effective ministers because of our experiences in the black church.

This book is not exhaustive. The qualities addressed do not tell the whole story of the black church experience. We could have written more. But at some point, we had to stop and simply publish the book.

Essentially, this book attempts to flip the script. The sometimes patronizing attitude of white Christians toward black Christians assumes superiority of method and ministry. So, this book parts the curtains and opens the window to a church world still foreign to the majority of white Christians.

The denomination that nurtured Bill and Joel began in 1845 when white Baptists from the South wanted to take their slaves with them to the mission field. The larger Baptist family would not permit it. The descendents of those folks formally apologized a few years ago, but too many whites still have a long, long way to go. Bill and Joel are no longer welcomed in that denomination, but our religious roots and heritage belong to it. Therefore, our hope is that this book takes another step on the historic road toward reconciling black and white Christians. We have witnessed strengths in the black church that whites need and testify here to those strengths.

—Bill & Joel

NOTES

1. Carl Jung, *Synchronicity: An Acausal Connecting Principle* (Princeton, NJ: Princeton University Press, 1973).

ACKNOWLEDGMENTS

We wish to acknowledge those whose collaboration and encouragement enabled the publication of this project. The friendship that the two of us have forged since 2002 has enriched and enlarged our circle of concern and our commitment to making a difference. We are on a journey, and we want to run on to see what the end will be.

We wish to thank Rev. Dr. J. Alfred Smith Sr. He has been a true friend to the both of us. This legendary man is pastor emeritus of Allen Temple Baptist Church in Oakland, California; an engaging professor at American Baptist Seminary of the West, part of the Graduate Theological Union, at Fuller Theological Seminary, and at Golden Gate Baptist Theological Seminary; a published author of numerous books; past president of the Progressive National Baptist Convention; and recipient of the Living Legend Award at the E. K. Bailey International Expository Preaching Conference. He has promoted this project from the beginning and has opened the door to Judson Press and to the publishing of our book, *What We Love About the Black Church: Can We Get a Witness*. His introduction to this work is humbling, and we hope to have lived up to the horizons drawn in the opening words. We are grateful beyond statement for his belief in the book and in us.

We wish to thank editor Rhoda McKinney-Jones, whose contribution to this project we cannot state in mere words. She has read our dialogues, has saved us from turning lemonade into lemons, and has helped us with our desire to, "First do no harm." She has entered into the vision of our concept, but ultimately she has entered our hearts. Her afterword catches all of the rays of the sun and magnifies them on one point—a love for the black church. We owe her a debt that only the response of the readers can repay. Her hand- and heartprints are on every page, and her spirit sweetens the atmosphere of the prose.

We also wish to acknowledge Rev. Dr. Aidsand Wright-Riggins III, executive director of National Ministries for American Baptist Churches USA and CEO of Judson Press, and Rev. Rebecca Irwin-Diehl, editor at Judson Press, who helped guide us on this journey. Judson, that historic and honored publication house, has truly taken this project to heart and has opened our private dialogue to the world.

Without doubt, we would also like to thank Rev. Dr. Ralph Douglas West Sr. of the Church Without Walls, whose presence in our lives, warmth of spirit in our fellowship, and ceaseless advocacy of all we are doing in this book, with the Bishop College renaissance, and with Proclaimers Place, makes us want to do our best.

We also wish to thank our schools and colleagues at Georgetown College, Baylor University, and George W. Truett Theological Seminary, specifically Baylor interim president and Truett dean, Rev. Dr. David E. Garland; Truett associate dean Rev. Dr. Dennis Tucker; and the board of trustees of Georgetown College. All have been perpetual sources of support and spiritual energy, and continue to encourage us to persevere.

Now, what can we say of those who have contributed their responses to each chapter? Some of them are new friends in the ministry, discovered in the preparation of this book. Others are brothers and sisters whose friendship and fellowship in the gospel we dearly treasure. They are loyal to the utmost, closer than life's next breath and companions in time and eternity.

And finally, we would like to thank our special partners in life and in ministry, Jan Banister Crouch and Joanne Michele Gregory. Their Christlike demeanors and spiritual characteristics are a daily amazement to us. More than anyone would know, they have enabled us to make this journey and travel this road in ministry, and we are the better for having been loved by them.

CHAPTER 1

PREACHING

Preach the word. (2 Timothy 4:2, NIV)

Rev. Dr. Gardner C. Taylor is the only pastor to win the Presidential Medal of Freedom. He has long been considered one of the most influential preachers of our time. Now in his nineties, he lives in Raleigh, North Carolina. For years, he had an ongoing national speaking schedule that would daunt many preachers half his age. His preaching career spans much of the past century, including a 42-year pastorate at the historic Concord Baptist Church of Christ in Brooklyn, New York.

He is a friend to presidents and kings and helped to form the Progressive National Baptist Convention with his friend, Rev. Dr. Martin Luther King Jr. In 1975–76 Dr. Taylor gave a series of lectures as a part of the Lyman Beecher Lectureship on Preaching at Yale University, the most noted of all preaching lecture series. He is beyond iconic.

To listen to him preach is to hear the ages, the pathos of history, and the voice of time. I have interviewed him extensively about the mysterious power of black preaching. He explains the black preacher in terms of the black experience in America. "Blacks are enough of a part of the total culture to understand it. Yet, they are enough apart from the total culture to see it from the side, from another angle. It is the experience of having one foot in the larger culture and one foot out of the larger culture that gives the unique angle of vision to the black preacher," Dr. Taylor said.

This is remarkable coming from a man who called President John F. Kennedy "Jack," and his brother Robert F. Kennedy "Bobby," and helped them in Brooklyn during the 1960 presidential campaign. That kind of perspective is perspective, indeed.

Another aspect of Dr. Taylor's preaching is the combination of warm, devotional commitment to the risen Christ in prayer and in trenchant pointed social commentary. I have never heard Dr. Taylor preach when he does not, on one hand, call us all to a commitment to Christ in a deeper and more profound way, while at the same time blow the trumpet for righting wrongs, helping the oppressed, and standing for justice. He truly preaches the Social Gospel.

In San Francisco in 2008, he preached on "The Song of Moses and the Song of the Lamb," from Revelation, chapters 4 and 5. From Revelation 4, he sounded—as only he could—the call for justice and liberation from oppression. Then, in a magnificent transition, he called us into the rarefied atmosphere of Revelation 5, "The Song of the Lamb," the transcendent worship at the throne of the Cosmic Christ. He married the horizontal and the vertical, the ethics and the theology, the great imperative of the Gospel and the great indicative that Christ has risen.

This has characterized all of his preaching. It is no truncated call to social action without a call to Christian consecration. He has modeled that this coupling is the secret of black preaching at its best.

BILL'S REFLECTION

The preaching of black pastors has always fascinated me. I remember as a child in Jackson, Mississippi, listening to the deep voices of African American civic leaders, most of whom were preachers. In seminary, I met a black minister named Carl Lee, and we had two things in common—basketball and preaching.

As the only person of color in my preaching class, he brought to the pulpit an energy and creativity that amazed me. I often asked him how he prepared sermons, so I inquired about his delivery. One day, he shared a secret with me that he called the "five gears," which involves modulating one's voice and pitch and sometimes speaking with a sense of urgency, all in an effort to engage the congregation while delivering God's word.

As a result of our friendship, I *thought* I had the inside scoop on how black preachers prepared their sermons. That is one reason I was so excited to be able to speak in November 2006 at Friendship-West Baptist Church, a phenomenal church in Dallas, Texas. The church's gifted pastor, Rev. Dr. Frederick D. Haynes III, a graduate of Bishop College, had invited the ministerial alumni of Bishop to gather for fellowship and to hear a proposal from Georgetown College about a new partnership.

I decided—attempted, really—to use the five gears. As I was ending my remarks, I began to move from fourth into fifth gear by announcing I was about to sit down but had one more thing to say. At the conclusion of my remarks, I received an enthusiastic response for my content; however, the master of ceremonies turned to me and said, "Dr. Crouch, your remarks were wonderful and exciting, but you need to know you will never be able to preach like a black man!" Ouch! And, yes, I learned a very valuable lesson—about myself and about black preaching.

The secret of black preaching is not the five gears. It involves much more than I have the ability to duplicate or explain. Black preaching uses energy and spirit to take the Word of God and bring it to life in a way that changes lives. It demands that the hearer listen, think, and respond. After traveling the country the last five years, listening to the sermons of these special communicators, I am a richer man for the journey.

JOEL'S REFLECTION

A member of the United Church of Canada and an astute observer of preaching, Dr. Paul Scott Wilson of the Emmanuel College at the University of Toronto has written extensively about the preaching experience. To explain the vitality of black preaching, he uses an interesting metaphor of the child's toy called the magic slate.

He comments that the biblical narrative is like that for the black preacher. For many in the majority culture, there is, at best, a translucent or sometimes opaque quality about the biblical narrative. In the black preaching experience, the preacher experiences the text with a transparency between the "then" of the text and the "now" of current circumstances.[1]

The Exodus is *now.* The prophet Amos cries out *today.* There is an immediacy of experience. The pastor does not have to cross an elaborate hermeneutical or homiletic bridge between then and now. The two are part of one seamless experience. On a given Sunday, the black preacher is Moses and the black congregation, the children of Israel. The Exodus is still being performed.

Over the last twenty years, the majority white church has rediscovered narrative preaching. The halls of academia researched the issue and declared that storytelling is good, and recounting the biblical narrative in vivid, colloquial English, with the smells, sounds, sights, and tactile realities, helps preaching to be more accessible and understandable.

While acknowledging that is a worthy discovery, I chuckled to think that white academic homiletes "discovered" what black theologians have known for centuries, long before their ancestors were slaves. Bible stories are powerful, retold just the way they are. An abiding power of black preaching is narrative, with its vivid, dramatic, uninhibited, and inventive recounting of the Bible.

Dr. Gardner Taylor once noted that oppressed people develop a capacity for imagination. He points to the black experience as well as to the Irish experience. The oppressed human spirit will find a creative outlet for expression. The unspeakable evil of slavery did yield some unexpected gifts to the black culture. One of them was the glorious capacity for preachers to frame biblical stories in a narrative that lights up a pulpit, lifts a congregation, and awakens hearts to the present power of God's ancient Word.

BILL'S REFLECTION

Rev. Dr. Willis Polk is a personal friend, pastor of Imani Baptist Church in Lexington, Kentucky, and a graduate of Georgetown College. He was delighted when I called him to make arrangements for my leadership students to attend his Sunday worship service. At that time, there were twenty-two students in our leadership program, only two of whom were people of color. It proved to be a day our students will never forget. They were introduced to "walking the offering," a remarkable choir, and a black preacher inspired by the Word of God. Later, after the worship service, Dr. Polk agreed to go to lunch (much later than the students were used to eating!) and to help our students understand the dynamics of the worship they had just experienced. It was a new and positive experience for everyone.

Dr. Polk is a serious expository preacher. There was no question that he was well prepared to open the Word and bring it to life in a way that would impact his congregation. His time in the pulpit was the high point of the service. His people followed the Word and responded in a vocal and affirming way. In the black church, the sermon is the moment when the pastor speaks directly to his or her people—and the people respond. Each pastor varies in his or her use of a well-prepared manuscript, but it is clear none is completely captive to written preparation—the Holy Spirit leads the sermonizing.

A current event, an experience in the life of a parishioner, an incident in the parking lot or narthex, or the mood of the praise and worship preliminaries can lead the pastor in a direction he or she had not anticipated. This movement, however, makes the Word even more relevant to the people who have gathered to hear a sermon of hope. It is during this time that the pastor calls the congregation to action in a very personal way. As their spiritual leader, the preacher is committed to helping parishioners in their righteous walk with the Lord.

After the service with Dr. Polk, our students asked many questions about sermon preparation time, his connection with the choir, and the freedom to occasionally let the Holy Spirit lead the service away from the printed program. When asked to identify the most important part of his ministry, he responded without hesitation: "the preaching of the Word in a relevant manner to my people."

I would think *all* preachers, regardless of race or denomination, would agree. But the black church preacher connects through a freedom of expression much different than I have seen in any other tradition.

RESPONSE FROM REV. DR. AL B. SUTTON JR.

Drs. Bill Crouch and Joel Gregory have astutely captured the essence of black preaching. Black preaching is special. It was forged in the crucible of American history through years of suffering and unimaginable struggle. It is a style that has been colored by passion and energy, clear thinking, an enormous concern for social justice, and a commitment to the least of these (Matthew 25:40).

Black preaching is characterized by an unashamed determination to preach Christ and his crucifixion. And much of this is couched, as Joel has indicated, in our love for the biblical narrative. We love to tell the story. And, if I might add, the genius of black preaching is our ability to tell the story.

We do seem to have a way of bringing the Word of God to life for our congregations that invites a response from our members. We preach to the oppressed, the disinherited, and they seem to identify uniquely with the minority culture in the Scriptures that spent much time as an occupied people.

We can identify with the captivity of the children of Israel in Egypt, with their wandering in the wilderness, and with their pursuit of the land of promise. We tend to identify with their human condition. When Joshua and the children of Israel arrived at the Jordan River and the waters had overflowed the banks, God miraculously made a way for them to get across. We could identify with that, because we as a people know something about impassable places and how God has made ways for us, when that way was not in sight.

Narrative preaching allows us to relive the biblical story for our members in ways that are very real and cogent. Storytelling not only colorfully informs our congregation while building suspense, it also sets the ground for transformation through a genuine encounter with the God of Scripture. Perhaps this is why, as Bill has indicated, black church preachers connect so well to their congregations because their sermons "demand that hearers listen, think, and respond."

RESPONSE FROM REV. DR. CYNTHIA L. HALE

I appreciate Drs. Bill Crouch and Joel Gregory's thoughtful and insightful assessment of the black preacher and the art of black preaching, because, while preaching is truly a gift ordained of God, it is an art—a prophetic one. The authors are on target with the assertion that black preaching is essentially energetic and creative, filled with pathos and passion, informed by the weight of our past.

Most theologians would readily agree that the black preacher has the ability to make the ancient yet relevant text come alive in ways that speak intimately to the hearer, affecting the heart and the mind and ultimately calling for a response and action from the listeners.

Dr. Gregory says, "An abiding power of black preaching is narrative, with its vivid, dramatic, uninhibited, and inventive recounting of the Bible." Black preaching at its finest, in the words of Dr. Crouch, "uses energy and spirit to take the Word of God and bring it to life in a way that changes lives. It demands that the hearer listen, think, and respond." I could not have said it better.

That is precisely, in my opinion, what makes black preaching distinctive, different, and an art form blessed by the Creator. Black preaching, while it is an intellectual experience of a well-thought-out and crafted argument for whatever theological thesis the preacher is making, is more than what appeals to one's brain. Black preaching at its best speaks to the head and the heart, the theoretical and the practical plus the emotional.

Black preaching speaks to the troubled soul and the downtrodden spirit—giving hope to those who have lost it, offering peace in life's storms, and unearthing joy in the midst of unspeakable sorrow. Black preaching speaks to hearers where they live, where they are in the moment, and where they move and have their beings. We make the historic text relevant to today's experience, transforming perspective, and so we transform the lives of hearers of the Word.

Okay, so why such an emphasis on transformation? That question remains. The answer is steeped in our history as a people. Black preaching is able to transform because of the distinctive perspective we bring to the primary subject of the preaching experience: God. Black preaching is concerned about a sovereign God who is intimately involved in the world but is also involved in the lives of God's people. Black preaching addresses the pain of the past, while giving hope that new days will dawn with joy and possibility.

Out of our historical and sociocultural experiences as African-ancestored people who have been oppressed and marginalized, we have a unique understanding of God and Christianity. Noted theologian Rev. Dr. Cleophus J. LaRue states in his book, *The Heart of Black Preaching:*

> As a result of their historical marginalization and struggle, what became most important to blacks in their encounters with Euro-American Christianity was not dogma or abstract theological reflection, but an intimate relationship with a powerful God who demonstrated throughout scripture a propensity to side with the downtrodden.[2]

The connection between the struggles of black folks and the God of Scripture makes what we do decidedly different. It allows the black preacher, with empathy and understanding, to present a God who is on the side of God's people, particularly those who are marginalized and struggling. We can do that, because as a people we know something about living on life's sharp edges.

A black preacher is set apart when he or she preaches about a God who not only cares, but also is able to work powerfully in and through situations to bring about change for the good of the listener. It is preaching about a sovereign God who acts in powerful and concrete ways to bring salvation, deliverance, healing, and whole-life prosperity, which causes hearers to "listen, think and respond."

Who wouldn't respond to a God like this?

✳ TAKEAWAYS

1. Rediscover preaching as the central task of ministry. Magnify the moment of proclamation.

2. Believe that on any given Sunday, preaching really does speak something to somebody. Never lose confidence that this day your words as a preacher may impact those seeking God.

3. Recover the power of vivid narrative preaching. Tell the story, and trust the story to do the work.

4. Be socially relevant, and make today's experience relate to God's directive.

NOTES

1. Paul Scott Wilson, *Preaching and Homiletical Theory* (St. Louis: Chalice Press, 2004), 105–8.

2. Cleophus J. LaRue, *The Heart of Black Preaching* (Louisville: John Knox Press, 1999), 3.

CHAPTER 2

ENCOURAGEMENT

*Let us encourage one another—and all
the more as you see the Day approaching.
(Hebrews 10:25, NIV)*

JOEL'S REFLECTION

Encouragement from the black church and its preachers provides one of the backdrops for my writing these reflections along with Bill. On a warm Texas September night in 1992, I resigned from one of the largest and most influential churches in the nation, First Baptist Church of Dallas. As a result of that decision, I moved from a huge home to a tiny apartment, from a large salary to no salary, from being on national television and radio to literally disappearing from the public eye.

The story is too long and complicated, and its details are not helpful to relate here.[1] Suffice it to say that more than seventeen years ago, I thought I had lost everything—including the support of my denomination and many colleagues whom I had counted as friends. That season in my life was personally devastating and vocationally crippling. I was sure my ministry was over, my preaching was finished, and the value of my three university degrees was worthless. The life I had lived from 1964 to 1992, from the age of sixteen to the age of forty-four, was essentially over. It was a low point.

Like the Hebrew patriarch Joseph, however, I did some things to myself and some things were done to me. Pride on Joseph's part, jealousy on his brothers' part, and unwise favoritism on Jacob's part all contributed to the saga of Joseph, told in Genesis 37. As in Joseph's story, my difficult situation made me wobble with spiritual vertigo. Human situations are seldom simple. Mine certainly was not.

But through it all, one minister kept calling me. The late Rev. Dr. E. K. Bailey, pastor of the Concord Missionary Baptist Church in Dallas, picked up his phone and called me again and again and again. He had no inherent reason to do so, other than the grace and bigness of his own heart. The conversations were always similar and warm: "God is not through with you. God did not give you what he gave you for you to stop. You must preach."

Frankly, I thought my kind friend meant well but had no idea the reality I was living. Yet, those calls to my tiny apartment gave me the oxygen of hope. He helped me to breathe. I did not dare believe his words of encouragement, but they held a glimmer of promise and possibility. Here was a black preacher holding out a life preserver to a white preacher who felt forgotten by his own faith community and abandoned by many he had known. Dr. Bailey became a healing balm.

The healing process started with that unfailing encouragement from my late friend Dr. Bailey and culminated in one more seemingly simple telephone call. Life, destiny, future, hope, and ministry all hung on the thin wire of that single call. At my lowest point, Dr. Bailey made a connection, when he called once more, not merely to speak more encouragement into my life but to issue an invitation.

Dr. Bailey called to ask me to preach at his International Expository Preaching Conference. I had no clue that by accepting his invitation, I would soon experience a most significant day in my life. I drove the thirty miles from Fort Worth, Texas, to the Fairmont Hotel in downtown Dallas. I was expecting a midsized seminar room occupied by a handful of preachers gathered to hear me reflect on what had happened in my recent departure from the pastorate. Instead, I walked into a grand ballroom filled with hundreds of black preachers. And it suddenly dawned on me that I had better *really* preach, if for no other reason than not to disappoint my friend, who at great risk and under withering criticism from my opponents had taken a chance on me.

God chose to visit that hour. It was God's sovereign choice, and I do not remember having another hour like it. Glory came down unexpectedly; I could not believe it. And when I was through, I was rushed by hundreds of black preachers. They embraced me, affirmed me, picked me up, validated me, and have never let me go.

Little country churches, megachurches, East Coast churches, West Coast churches, Chicago churches, Florida churches, and Louisiana Bayou churches have asked me to preach. I cannot pretend to understand it.

My ability to cross what many thought was an unbridgeable chasm of race is and was an act of God alone. The whole thing took on its own life. My life, ministry, and destiny changed on May 26, 1998, in a Fairmont Hotel ballroom in downtown Dallas. I will forever be grateful.

The day before Dr. Bailey died, I sat by his bed in Methodist Dallas Medical Center in the Oak Cliff area of Dallas. He could not talk above a whisper. I looked into his glazed eyes and, with tears streaming from mine, I thanked him, said how much I loved him and that I owed him everything. There was the hint of a smile on his face. The next day he was in heaven.

BILL'S REFLECTION

When Joel and I began this journey together, he predicted I would find more encouragement than I had ever experienced in my career. I paid attention because Joel had many more years of relating to black men and women of God than I did. I had no idea of what Joel meant, but I certainly was eager to learn.

Now, five years down the road, I know Joel to be a truth-teller. My experience with black preachers has given me a level of encouragement way beyond anything I have ever known, and the foundation of that encouragement, I believe, is trust.

I was fortunate to be able to have a level of credibility among some black preachers, because Joel told them I was trustworthy. I could, of course, lose that trust, but I began on a high note. From the first meeting I ever had with a group of African American church leaders, until today, I have been overwhelmed with encouragement, not only professionally, but also personally.

Sitting in a large conference room in Nashville, Tennessee, in November 2005, I met for the first time with the four national black Baptist convention presidents. It was one of the highlights of my life to sit in a room with men who represented 7.6 million Baptists all over the world. Rev. Dr. Stephen Thurston, Rev. Dr. Melvin Von Wade, Rev. Dr. William J. Shaw, and Rev. Dr. Major Jemison sat across from Joel and me and listened to our proposal for a partnership with Georgetown College designed to keep the spirit and legacy of Bishop College Alive.

Joel affirmed his blessing of my plan, and the others listened intently and agreed to move forward. I was ecstatic, but the real joy has come during the days since then. These four men have become my friends and great encouragers. I receive calls, letters, and invitations from them. They enjoy making fun of me whenever it is appropriate! And whenever our paths cross, I am always treated as a seasoned friend.

JOEL'S REFLECTION

After I left my church and wandered alone, the other black minister who adopted me was Rev. Dr. B. R. Daniels Sr., of Beth Eden Missionary Baptist Church in Fort Worth, Texas. When it seemed few people in Texas could find me, Dr. Daniels somehow did and asked that I meet with a group of ministers. He invited me to talk about my experience, my future, and my autobiography. That group of black pastors gathered around, embraced, encouraged, and simply listened to me.

What Dr. Daniels did after that initial meeting was even more amazing. He asked me to preach at his church on an Easter Sunday morning. I could not believe it. This esteemed pastor invited me into his house of worship on one of the holiest of days in the Christian calendar. It is a relationship that continues to this day; for eleven years, I have held a Passion Week revival and have preached on Easter Sunday at his church.

The experience with Dr. Daniels was the first of hundreds of affirmations by my brothers and sisters of color from all over the nation. After I left the pastorate, experienced a divorce, and worked in a secular job, the majority of white Christians in those first difficult years of the mid-1990s did not know what to do with me. There were a few who stuck with me and remained my friends, but only a few.

The majority culture could accept neither my leaving a legendary church nor my losing a marriage. To have both happen within the same two years truly sidelined me from ministry in white churches. Only now that I am teaching and have received the validation of white institutions of higher learning, it is interesting to experience a renewal of ministry among whites. Those white friends have come to validate me in time. For that I am profoundly grateful.

The fact remains, however, that my black brothers and sisters embraced me immediately after my losses and have not stopped encouraging me, and for that I owe a debt of gratitude. I am humbled by the black church's willingness to show great grace in accepting people where they are. They act on the belief that grace really does work, that God does not abandon us because of difficulties. As my brothers and sisters have reminded me so often, "The gifts and calling of God are without repentance" (Romans 11:29, KJV).

I have pondered for years why this quality of gracious compassion and encouragement is so often found in black culture. My conclusion is that oppressed people have an abiding sense of empathy with those in life's low places. When people live out of grace themselves, they extend grace to others. Jesus said that the one who has been forgiven much, loves much, and I have seen also that those who have suffered much, encourage much. Out of our own experiences of trial and pain, we discover new depths of compassion and new ability to encourage others.

BILL'S REFLECTION

Rev. Dr. David L. Boyle Sr., pastor of Antioch Baptist Church in Whiteville, Tennessee, and another Bishop College graduate, is a remarkable encourager. The first time I met Dr. Boyle, I felt warmth and a genuine interest in me. He was interested in who I was and the message I had to give. I remember being in the den of one of his Bishop College classmates, sharing my dream of how Georgetown College and Bishop College alumni could partner together. God has blessed Dr. Boyle with a big smile, and he uses that smile to beam encouragement across any room. That is what he did for me that day. The more I talked, the more he smiled. I felt supported and affirmed.

Since that gathering, Dr. Boyle and I have become very good friends, so much so that he entrusted his son to me as a student at Georgetown College. His daughter and I have engaged in regular conversations about her graduate-school dreams. Often Dr. Boyle will call my cell phone to offer words of encouragement and to pray for me. Those simple acts let me know that he sincerely cares.

Yes, we met because of my position as a college president, but our relationship has become so much more than that today—it is about love as brothers in Christ. Now, I try to return what Dr. Boyle and other black pastors like him have given me. I call their cells to say hello, to have a word of prayer, to seek advice about diversity efforts of Georgetown College, and to receive an uplifting of my spirit from them. These men are always encouraging and providing support in any way they can.

They have opened doors for me and have volunteered to assist in other ways. I now have two African American pastors on my board of trustees. On occasion, each will call just to let me know that in their quiet moments, they lifted a prayer for me. They ask about my wife, Jan, and our children. Then they ask if there are any specific prayer requests for our family. These calls don't last more than a few minutes, but my spirits are lifted every time. I am grateful these men have come into my life.

RESPONSE FROM REV. DR. MAURICE WATSON

Joel Gregory and Bill Crouch have underscored an aspect of the African American religious experience that is a part of the woof and warp of our churches. Encouragement is a theme that is threaded throughout the fiber of black church life. Consequently, I was not surprised to read their reflections of the high level of encouragement they received through their interaction with African American Christians.

Historically, the African American church has always been a source of encouragement and hope for its people. Our forefathers and -mothers were able to survive the atrocities of slavery because of the role the black church played in encouraging them to believe that "a better day is coming." Their circumstances were unbearable, but the message of encouragement they heard through their church experience helped them to survive.

The late Dr. E. K. Bailey and other black pastors gave Joel Gregory that same kind of encouragement. When facing the darkest hour of his life, a black pastor essentially told Joel his ministry was not over because "better days are coming." That's vintage black church encouragement! It says, "If you fall down because of your own doing, or if you are pushed down by the hands of others, you don't have to stay down. You can get back up again!"

What was it that helped Joel rise from the mat of despair and get back into the ring of effective ministry? It was the loving encouragement he received from black Christians, who not only preach grace but practice grace and unconditional love.

Bill Crouch discovered what it means to be encouraged through new and meaningful relationships with African American ministers. The relationships he has developed with black pastors, black students, and the students' parents gelled and became solid through mutual respect and trust. Knowing the genuine passion that Bill has for increasing the educational opportunities of African American students on the campus of Georgetown College, it is a compliment to him that he has been able to sustain and build on those new friendships.

The black church has been, for many, a safety net, a crucible of caring for those who have been rejected. Encouragement is our legacy and one of the foundations on which many of us have modeled our ministries. It is a gift our history has given us.

RESPONSE FROM REV. JEWEL M. LONDON

Dr. Gregory and Dr. Crouch have experienced the epitome of encouragement in the African American church. That encouragement is neither feigned nor contrived, but rather it is a natural reaction to the love of Christ that embodies the very essence of our institution.

Reflecting on Dr. Gregory's observance that "when people have been oppressed, they have an abiding sense of empathy with someone in life's low places" reminds me of the words of the late Rev. Dr. Martin Luther King Jr., who said, "The ultimate measure of a man is not where he stands in moments of comfort and convenience, but where he stands at times of challenge and controversy."[2]

The African American culture has suffered great oppression, and with oppression came severe loss and lack of opportunity. But as a people, we have continued to maintain our generosity of spirit and have been willing to extend great grace and unending compassion to others.

This is the beauty of the African American church, incessantly giving and demonstrating God's love, joy, and hope to all who enter her doors. We are that forever tower of refuge and safe haven for our community. This amazing body of believers has proven time and time again that it is a forgiving institution that embraces those who have nowhere else to turn.

Dr. Gregory's encounter with the late Rev. Dr. E. K. Bailey reminded me of a dark season in my own life. While going through a tumultuous journey of rejection and rediscovery, God sent one source of encouragement after another to directly impact my voyage. He used wonderful community leaders within my sphere, both black and white—such as Dr. Earline O. Allen, Rev. Cheryl Young Archer, Superintendent John Banks, Elder James Strolger, Rev. Dr. Barbara Wright, and others—to encourage me and serve as pillars of support.

They pushed, pulled, embraced, and undergirded me with words of wisdom, instruction, and countless prayers during a painful season, when I was not permitted to preach or to administer the ordinances of the church. These leaders, like Dr. Bailey for Dr. Gregory, helped me to breathe. With relentless dedication, they encouraged me to pursue, hear, and obey the voice of God while waiting patiently for God's providence to prevail. And so it did. In due season, in God's perfect timing, validation was confirmed, and as with Dr. Gregory, I experienced a renewal of ministry.

As Dr. Crouch experienced, true encouragement does not stop with an introduction and a handshake; it continues until the meter in a person's heart says the work is done. The pastors whom Crouch and Gregory encountered proved themselves as God's ministers in deed beyond their titles. I have found this dedication to be true in most African American pastors, who give from the cores of their beings. The African American church as a whole carries this same sentiment, and it continues to pour out the love of Christ to those who have been fortunate to be chosen recipients of its grace—for what we have *freely* received, we *freely* give.

❊ Takeaways

1. Embrace those who have hit life's hardest places. You never know when they will reciprocate when you need the same encouragement and uplifting.

2. Leave judgment to others and to God. There will always be plenty of judges, but few encouragers.

3. Commit to reaching out and lifting up someone different every day. You will be blessed in the process.

NOTES

1. The full story of my history may be found in my earlier book, Joel Gregory, *Too Great a Temptation: The Seductive Power of America's Super Church* (Fort Worth, TX: Summit Group, 1994).

2. Martin Luther King Jr., *Strength to Love*, 1963. http://www.quotations page.com/quotes/Martin_Luther_King_Jr. (accessed February 18, 2010).

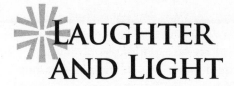LAUGHTER AND LIGHT

Then our mouth was filled with laughter, and
our tongue with shouts of joy. (Psalm 126:2)

BILL'S REFLECTION

Life is serious business. People hurt. People are afraid. People are oppressed. People die. People are poor, lonely, and sick. The African American community has scars from four hundred years of this seriousness. Yet, there is laughter, storytelling, encouragement, and, yes, joy in the midst of what could be pain. Laughter can be a balm. There truly is a balm in Gilead that heals the soul.

On this journey, I have discovered the joy of fellowship. On two separate occasions in the fall of 2009, I invited thirty African American pastors from the central Kentucky area to the Georgetown College president's house, my home, for dinner. The joy they had in seeing each other, the stories they told about each other, and the jabs they took at one another, amazed me. All I could do was to sit back, laugh, smile, and soak in the experience and the joy that came with this Christian fellowship.

Rev. Dr. C. B. Akins Sr. is pastor of the First Baptist Church Bracktown in Lexington, Kentucky. I have developed great admiration for him over the years, and I am delighted we are providing Georgetown College scholarships for five young men in his congregation so they may earn college degrees.

One summer Saturday morning, Dr. Akins was driving through Georgetown's campus when he saw me walking toward my office. He pulled up in his car, wanting to know what a college president was doing working on a Saturday morning. Then he asked directions to a meeting that was taking place on our campus. Confidently, I told him where the meeting was being held. He drove off, following my directions. A few minutes later, it occurred to me that I had sent him to the wrong location. Trying to recover, I called our security officers and had them find the misplaced pastor to redirect him! Later I met up with him at the meeting to apologize. But, I stayed long enough to have him publicly tell the audience that they should watch out for college presidents who can lead you astray, even on their own campuses. The audience roared with laughter at his verbal jab and his ability to put a college president in his place. Message delivered. I understood, and it was a great moment; laughter was the equalizer.

JOEL'S REFLECTION

Absolutely. As an itinerant preacher in dozens of black churches annually, I spend a great deal of worship and free time in the company of black ministers. Nothing gets in the way of celebration, joy, good humor, chuckles, chortles, and belly laughs for long. In the face of difficulty, changed plans, missed schedules, awful confusions, disappointing speakers, unexpected interruptions, and outright provocations that accompany church life in any culture, my friends of color will find the humor and joy and will celebrate it.

Take Rev. Dr. Joe Carter, senior pastor of New Hope Baptist Church in Newark, New Jersey. Downtown Newark is hardly a setting confused with good times. Dr. Carter has often acted as a peacemaker between the rival gangs, sometimes putting his own life on the line. Yet, spend twenty-four hours with Dr. Carter and his staff, and one cannot help but find the joy.

On one occasion, Dr. Carter told his congregation he is going to give me personal whooping lessons in the sanctuary. (For the uninitiated, whooping is the preacher's musical intonation often heard at the end of many black sermons.)

On another of my visits, he took me to a local Italian restaurant that looked suspiciously like a place featured in the former HBO series, *The Sopranos*. The old Italian owner cussed Dr. Carter out for bringing me in and cussed me out for being from Texas. Disregarding the hostility, disrespect, and regional prejudice of the interaction, Dr. Carter and I found humor and grace in the irony of a man who could have been chosen by central casting for an old-school Mafia movie cussing out two preachers, one black and one white.

Dr. Carter and his late brother, Rev. Ron Carter, showed me once and for all the inventiveness of black preachers having fun. I took them to the Crowne Plaza Invitational Golf Tournament at Colonial Country Club in Fort Worth, Texas, a place with very few ebony faces. They eased the racial tension with a stunt on the eighth green that I could have never conceived. Rev. Joe Carter called his church in Newark and told them to turn the television station to CBS. He then told them to listen for his brother to shout the perennial, "It's in the hole!" just as Phil Mickelson putted on the par three. With the cell phone to his ear, Joe burst out in gales of laughter as he listened to Ron's shout, delayed a few seconds but clearly heard on his cell phone from a television in Newark. While everyone else cheered Phil's putt, we fell out at the thought of Ron's interesting golf comment circling the planet!

BILL'S REFLECTION

Not long ago, Brian Evans, executive director of the Office of Diversity at Georgetown College, and I attended the Progressive National Baptist Convention in Washington, DC. We organized a small gathering of Bishop College graduates to join us so we could update them on our Bishop College Alive Project. Whenever these Bishop alums get together, there is remorse for losing their college, but after a few minutes those laments turn to oft-told stories and lots of laughter.

At the gathering, they talked of dorms that lacked air conditioning in the summer and had no heat in the winter, of gruff professors and faculty, of college pranks, young-preacher pressures, high expectations, and promises kept and broken. The stories, I am sure, were embellished and have grown and expanded with time, but before Brian and I knew it, we had been listening and laughing for almost two hours.

Now, I know my white friends and pastors will say this kind of storytelling is no different than when we get together to remember our college days and lost youth. But there is a distinct difference. Our colleges still exist. Bishop College is no longer. The pain and anger of that loss have occasionally turned to laughter, an expressed joy for having had the experience of being in that place at that time. My experience cannot compare.

It is remarkable how black men and women of the faith truly believe God's Word and know that God has come to give us life, and life more abundantly. Out of life's tragedies, we can have faith that all things work together for the good, for those who love our Lord. That's why our friends of color can laugh freely, deeply, and with incredible sincerity.

JOEL'S REFLECTION

The distinguished pastor, Rev. Dr. Ralph Douglas West Sr. of the Church Without Walls in Houston, Texas, was sometimes a guest in my condominium when I was single. On one occasion when he was visiting with his brother, my clothes dryer needed to be repaired, leaving me with no way of drying laundry. The three of us found a rather woebegone Laundromat around 11 p.m. and started sticking clothes and bedding into four dryers. While the clothes dried, we went to a shop next door to have a cup of coffee and talk homiletics. Close to midnight, a woman in the coffee shop recognized Dr. West from his television ministry. Then a man recognized me from some Texas Baptist venue. And finally, two of our students who were in the corner recognized us both.

Obviously, there was great discussion about what a pastor of a black megachurch was doing with me, a white theologian, in a Laundromat washing sheets, towels, and some unmentionables. They had questions, and they had plenty of jokes.

Truthfully, I know very few friends who would have gone with me to the Laundromat close to midnight, and virtually none who would have found the humor in being recognized. Yet, my African American brothers in the faith responded to the experience with gales of laughter. Then we relived it—the broken dryer, the wet bedding and underwear, getting recognized—and we wondered what those who saw us really thought and the tabloid-like rumors that could have ensued. So, we continued to laugh. What else could we have done?

Time after time across the country, I have had similar experiences with my brothers and sisters of color. Without exception, the most bizarre circumstances can provoke humor in situations that, in other cultures, might normally create frustration, even anger. There is a remarkable resilience in a culture that can see the irony and humor in the ridiculous and unexpected, and can transform the moment into laughter.

This experience I value as highly as any other in my interaction with black ministers. The white ministerial culture desperately needs the ability not to take itself so seriously. My decade of preaching and fellowshipping with ministers of color in humor and laughter has been the most healing time in my life. It has been both restorative and redemptive.

RESPONSE FROM **REV. DENNY D. DAVIS**

There is a time for everything—a time to weep and a time to laugh (Ecclesiastes 3:4). Humor is very prevalent in African American churches, as well as in other churches. Many times laughter is inspired by the pastor's personality. The pastor can prompt the congregation to laugh as a means to inspire lighthearted fellowship. Laughter is a means by which the pastor relates to parishioners, with the intent to personalize a common and calming connection. Proverbs 15:13 says, "A glad heart makes a cheerful countenance, but by sorrow of heart the spirit is broken."

Laughter is used to lift the spirits of worshippers as they participate in fellowship, so when they reflect on the time spent in service they will have a pleasant and positive memory. People come to church to be inspired and challenged to live out the fullness of their potential in the world.

Many times, life's challenges can cause one to become withdrawn, shut down, and cut off. For example, a pastor may use a humorous approach to sing the birthday song, rendering it in the most entertaining way to break the ice of isolation between members and to celebrate each other's significance. Jesus gave his Sermon on the Mount to express the blessed life, and he states in Luke 6:21, "Blessed are you who weep now, for you will laugh." The pastor's ability to laugh with the parishioners provides a sense of connection for members.

Worship should always have a theological focus with a therapeutic approach. One of the goals of church is to help us understand God and who we are in the light of God. Worship provides a source of help and healing for the soul. And laughter can be a means of healing, as stated in Proverbs 17:22, "A cheerful heart is a good medicine, but a downcast spirit dries up the bones." Laughter can be a balm.

Laughter can also be used as political satire, to drive home an important and poignant point in a non-confrontational and non-threatening way. It can make the truth of a bitter and tortured reality less painful, even if just for a moment. As African American people, we know about that reality, for we live it each and every day.

In short, life is serious business, and some humor along the way helps add spice. Laughter enables us to relieve stress and make it through the day. The text-messaging generation of our times has created a language of abbreviations to express ideas in a concise way. LOL is one often used, which simply means "Laugh Out Loud." So take time to laugh—God ordained it.

RESPONSE FROM REV. PAMELA R. RIVERA

The church is the place where the black community can come together weekly to hear a word from the Lord, listen to soul-stirring songs of hope and assurance, and share the experiences of the past week with other Christian brothers and sisters. Historically, the church is the unofficial designated pulse of the black community. The church is also the spiritual triage center that welcomes the troubled mind, the wounded spirit, and the lonely heart.

God is the Great Physician, and the pastor serves as a medical resident, with the gargantuan task of administering a timely remedy that is soothing, gender and age sensitive, easy to ingest, and God-prescribed to every attentive mind in attendance. Proverbs 17:22 says, "A cheerful heart is a good medicine, but a downcast spirit dries up the bones." Laughter, then, is an equal-opportunity, cross-cultural, biblical tonic available to all Christian communities that can be used as a salve to counteract life's emotional woes.

In the black church, the pastor defines the personality of the congregation. If the pastor is jovial, the congregation has the propensity to be jovial, and humor may be one of the central remedies used to break the ice, interrupt the mundane, or lighten a heavy load.

The worship experience is one of the few places where every human emotion can be experienced in one form or another in succession. After witnessing a sister shout herself out of her big-brim hat in response to the choir's soul-stirring rendition of "Amazing Grace," or listening to the life-changing testimony of a young black man who just gave his life to Christ, how can one break out into spontaneous, side-splitting laughter at such a time as this? But in our tradition, laughter is not always expressed in articulated sounds accompanied by facial expressions and bodily movements. It is more than that. Laughter is an expression of joy, satisfaction, agreement, and acknowledgment.

In any given black worship experience, laughter may manifest itself in the form of an ear-to-ear grin which serves as a silent statement of affirmation or acknowledgment. It may be expressed through a sudden shift from a seated position to a joyous leap, mimicking a child bouncing on a pogo stick. Laughter may also be disguised as a rhythmic handclap or a synchronized toe-tap. Laughter, for us, is more than just articulated sounds.

Laughter is only one way the black church celebrates and acknowledges God's redemptive power and saving grace, but such laughter is embedded in the black worship experience because we are an emotional and expressive people. Psalm 107:2 says, "Let the redeemed of the Lord say so, those he redeemed from trouble."

TAKEAWAYS

1. Look for the joy and laughter in ridiculous situations you encounter as a minister of the gospel. Many are like the weather; you cannot change them, so just enjoy the moment and laugh.
2. When you find yourself taking things too seriously, stop and find something ironic or humorous in the situation.
3. Lighten the load and pain of those around you by finding the humor in their situations and helping them to see it.
4. Humor heals and is contagious; pass it on and pay it forward.

CHAPTER 4

Mentoring Ministers:
The Next Generation

And what you have heard from me through
many witnesses entrust to faithful people who will
be able to teach others as well. (2 Timothy 2:2)

Bill's Reflection

How should aspiring ministers prepare for the role of pastor in a local church? Conventional white tradition places ministerial students in seminaries for a period of academic study and spiritual formation. Many of these students become so-called seminary pastors of small rural churches, a tradition that thrusts the seminarian or new graduate into a practical ministry setting alone. While most seminaries do require a minimum number of hours of supervised field ministry, that supervisory relationship is typically short-term and limited to institutionally required feedback.

Such limited exposure to oversight from more experienced professionals stands in stark contrast with other vocations. Medical students cannot receive their coveted degrees without being mentored for years in a hospital setting. Law students, shepherded by more knowledgeable attorneys, must have some moot-court experience. Future educators are usually required to complete a full year of student teaching before being certified by the state to teach our children and youth.

So it is in the black church. While African American ministers-in-training may have gone to seminary and may be working toward higher degrees, I have learned that few fail to be mentored under the guidance of an experienced senior pastor, whether in a formal or informal manner.

For lack of a better word, let us call these ministers-in-training the mentees. They are the "sons and daughters" of ministers or of a particular church. Larger black churches may have a number of such ministers handling official responsibilities in order to gain on-the-job experience and enhance the church's ministries. The relationship between the pastor and the minister-in-training may have occurred naturally, through a previously established relationship, or in a more formal way, where the younger charge seeks out guidance and mentoring.

Some mentees are former executives, second-career ministers, or students straight out of seminary who become associates of the senior pastor. The academic work of those in training may be through seminaries that are part of prestigious divinity schools or through smaller Bible colleges. Whatever the source of their academic training, ministers-in-training have a consistent intentionality to combine practical apprenticeship with academics, all wrapped around a deep spiritual commitment to further God's kingdom.

There is something to be learned and garnered from this model. Ministry is a hands-on profession, and the African American pastor has made incredible strides to develop and minister to the next generation in a very personal way.

JOEL'S REFLECTION

The African American pastor often faces a double challenge in mentoring. On one hand, the pastor mentors those who are newly ordained or being shaped for ordination in vocational ministry. This may be an organic function from inside a local church, or it may be a requirement of the denomination in a more formal process.

On the other hand, the pastor mentors in the more general arena of lay leadership in the church. There is a particularly great effort to support and develop young African American men in the contemporary black church—and in the community at large, for that matter, where too many young black men are being lost to criminality, early parenthood, and other risk-laden behaviors.

So, the African American male pastor not only functions as preacher, teacher, and father, but also as a model and symbol for Christian maleness and manhood. In that regard, the male African American pastor carries two burdens: one of officially shepherding ministers-in-training and another of being a role model for men who need mentoring in their walk toward Christian manhood. (Similarly, if without the same level of social urgency perhaps, African American female pastors mentor young women on their Christian trek toward womanhood.)

Traditionally, the mentees and ministers-in-training who are working in the church fulfill whatever role the senior pastor assigns. Coupled with seminary training, they may attend formal classes developed by the pastor or the denomination. Or their roles may include pinch-hitting for the pastor if a church has multiple locations or services, standing in when the pastor is out of town, visiting the sick, participating in the order of worship, serving communion, or traveling with the pastor to conventions.

Often the mentees or associates report directly to the pastor. While some churches may be more structured in terms of hierarchy, there is usually no multilayered, corporate chain of command, even in the largest of churches. The relationship between the pastor as mentor and the mentee-in-training can be direct and immediate, a true one-on-one.

Rev. Dr. Clifford Ashe III of DaySpring Ministries in Middletown, Pennsylvania, entered the pastorate from the corporate world, after having been mentored by Dr. Willie Richardson Sr. of Christian Stronghold Baptist Church in Philadelphia for a number of years. Now, Rev. Ashe mentors a group of men at DaySpring, implementing the model that he learned from Dr.

Richardson. Rev. Ashe's associates not only serve the church, but also assist at his annual Mighty Men of Valor Conference.

BILL'S REFLECTION

Another powerful example is the mentoring provided by the late Rev. Dr. E. K. Bailey to his many "sons in the ministry." When he observed potential and the calling on someone's life, he would seek God's guidance about the individual. If he felt led, he would begin to invest his time into the life of that "son." It was a life-time commitment.

Dr. Bailey's widow, Dr. Sheila Bailey, told me that many times family dinners were interrupted by the needs of a "son" seeking advice or encouragement. In fact, someone who was being mentored often occupied the spare bedroom in the Baileys' home. Those encounters included prayer, counseling, and church strategy, as well as very direct conversations about expectations and responsibilities. Well before the concept of accountability circles became popular, Dr. Bailey was practicing a version with his many "sons."

Rev. Leonard Leach, now pastor of Mt. Hebron Missionary Baptist Church in Garland, Texas, and Rev. Dr. Major L. Jemison of St. John Missionary Baptist Church of Oklahoma City, Oklahoma, are just two of Dr. Bailey's many sons in ministry. Each tells countless stories of the investment Dr. Bailey made in his life, leading him, providing opportunities, holding him accountable, and placing him in areas of responsibility that Dr. Bailey felt would mold and shape him into God's well-prepared servant.

My father, Dr. William Henry Crouch Sr., pastored three churches spanning a period of fifty years. And over the course of his ministry, he helped shepherd at least forty men and women through their calls to the Gospel of Jesus Christ. He prayed regularly and often for these young ministers, encouraging them on their paths. Today, he is eighty-two years old and has been retired for twelve years. Rarely, since his retirement, have his sons and daughters in the faith reached out to him. From my understanding and experience, that would not be the case in the black church.

Not long ago, Dr. Jemison shared with me one of his personal heartaches: Dr. Jemison's father in the ministry, Dr. E. K. Bailey, had died before Dr. Jemison's inauguration as president of the Progressive National Baptist Convention. "Dr. Bailey invested so much in me, I wanted him to see the fruit of his labor in my election," Dr. Jemison said. Men and women all over the country share these feelings about their mentors in the ministry. Mentoring is one of the most powerful aspects of the black church experience, because it pays forward, making an impact for generations.

JOEL'S REFLECTION

The relationship between the mentor and his or her protégé usually does not stop when the associate accepts a pastorate or a position at another fellowship. It continues as a lifetime bond of confidence, counsel, contact, and camaraderie. I have heard numerous African American preachers talk about the calls made and received on Saturday evenings before preaching and on Sunday nights after services, a kind of national networking of calls, reports, reviews, and evaluations that takes place in the black church culture.

My sense is that black pastors do not live in the same kind of isolation that many white preachers seem to suffer. Without overstating the situation, I have observed that after seminary, many, if not most, white preachers lose the ties with their original mentors in the church and academy. We seem to go off as free agents, entrepreneurs of church life without a superior, peer, or subordinate. In a word, we are and we act alone.

Not so in the black church culture. There is a commitment to connection. For example, riding to and from church to preach for black ministers, I have overheard hundreds of conversations between the pastors and those they mentor. Words of encouragement and practical assistance seem to be offered all the way to the pulpit. There is a sense, not only locally but nationally, that each Sunday "we are in this together."

I have never experienced that sense of camaraderie while preaching for the white church. Ministry in the majority church culture seems much lonelier. Although my mentors poured insights into me, including some of the very words I say in the pulpit today, I never dreamed of speaking to my mentors before or after preaching. Maybe they would have appreciated it, but I cannot say. That kind of relationship did not exist.

What I can note is a lifetime bond between mentors and mentees in the African American church experience. It is not unusual for a mentor to take members of his or her congregation, choir, deacon body, and ministerial staff to the church of a son or daughter in the ministry for a special occasion.

Every September at the invitation of Rev. Dr. N. L. Robinson Sr., pastor of Mt. Olive Baptist Church in Arlington, Texas, I preach at his church's revival. On that Sunday every year, the entire church body is invited to go in the afternoon with the ministers to another Texas town to celebrate the anniversary of the pastor's mentee. I could report similar such ventures in many black churches where I have preached and have observed church life.

For our black brothers and sisters in the faith, the old song by John Fawcett, "Blessed Be the Tie that Binds,"[1] is more than a song. It is a lifestyle.

RESPONSE FROM REV. DR. DONALD HILLIARD JR.

Drs. Crouch and Gregory have made some salient points about mentoring and its significance in the African American church. Mentoring ensures the succession of the next generation or church leaders, and for that reason, it is truly an everyday part of my ministry. My experience as pastor and mentor has been of priest, protector, and provider. Mentoring, while a necessary and much-needed endeavor, is not always easy. It takes commitment and focus, fidelity and follow-through. Today, we tend to be an incredibly self-absorbed and distracted people, consumed with

YouTube, Twitter, and text messaging. While we have become more technologically savvy, we are becoming less touchable and tactile, less personally connected and communal—and ultimately less open to hands-on guidance.

So, in this high-tech, fast-paced society, the notion of mentoring can get lost, like e-mails in cyberspace. We are so often in pursuit of the biggest, brightest, and largest—anything, rather than seeking counsel from a mother or father in the faith. We are fortunate as pastors if the Lord has blessed us with a son or daughter in ministry. As I pen this, I am celebrating my twenty-sixth pastoral anniversary and cannot help but think of my many sons and daughters, both in my local church and abroad, who are successfully practicing ministry.

Some serve as pastors to churches that are exact models of the Cathedral, our local church. Others have gathered what they found most attractive and have merged those elements into new ministries, while others have cast their vision into new territory. My job was never to create duplicates, clones, or mini-mes. My goal has been and continues to be to provide a guiding and faithful hand. I pray that I am successful in achieving this goal.

I am paternal by nature, a caregiver with an open heart. I love deeply and fully, and at times that can get in the way, being both a blessing and a curse. The blessing: There are those sons and daughters in the faith who have grown, have been prayed over, and have been sent forth into ministries, and the tie that binds remains tight, firm, loving, and loyal. But that love, loyalty, and caring can be challenged and sometimes shattered. Then there are those who have sought their own paths, not to adhering to advice that was given. In those cases, they are still my sons and daughters, but I must be pastoral enough to receive them no matter how far I feel they have strayed.

The biological daughters I helped my wife usher into the world often tell me, "Dad, you are so 'over,'" meaning that sometimes I can love too much, press too hard, and hold on too tight. As mentors, fathers, and mothers, we want those we are shepherding to succeed, but we often make the mistake of trying to mold them in our own image, rather than letting God do the shaping. These are the gifts and pains of mentoring.

As African American mentors, it is important to teach those who are young in ministry about authentic preaching, issues of social justice, and prophetic witnessing. Those things are extremely important and are at the crux of ministry. But it is equally important for mentors to model a complete ministry, including the cracks of hard realities.

In the African American tradition, we model not only while we are preaching and teaching, but also while we are reaching. Some things are caught and not taught. For example, some of the young men who travel with me and serve as drivers and adjutants have gained much knowledge from those backroom, late-at-night conversations where guards are dropped and raw humanity bubbles to the surface. Even in raw humanity, honesty abundant and foibles visible, the mentor can be an example of balance.

Such behind-the-scenes, everyday-life interactions are an opportunity to show what it means to preach and practice ministry, but they are also an opportunity to demonstrate what it means to be a Christian mother or father, husband or wife. In the African American tradition, not only is the preacher modeling the preaching gift and his or her own pastoral style, that minister is also modeling a personal lifestyle. That can be a challenge. In order for us to continue to give birth and nurture a generation of young men and women willing to serve this present age, it's imperative for preachers to model behavior God would deem worthy. That is not always easy.

The black church has long maintained that God-given gifts make room for you (see Proverbs 18:16, KJV), but character can keep you where you are. As I travel the country, what appears to be lacking with the faith's sons and daughters is the development of character. Yes, ouch. My own pastor, Dr. Kelmo Porter Jr., who baptized me when I joined St. John's Baptist Church as a fourth-generation AME, is my father in ministry. At eighty years old, bent over from wear, forgetful yet brilliant, scholarly and loving, he is still loyal to his ministry's sons and daughters.

He taught me the importance of submitting to his mantle. I learned from him not only what it means to be lifted and praised, but also what it means to be humbled. And I owe a debt of gratitude for all the guidance given by my apostolic father and consecrating bishop, Dr. John R. Bryant. Their lessons I hold onto as I attempt to guide those with whom God has blessed me. These sons and daughters in ministry carry, I pray, a part of what I tried to model and, yet, they have shaped their own molds.

All fathers want their children to soar but also struggle to let them go. My wife and I have three daughters, all in their twenties. I have relished and marveled at how they have grown into incredible young women. It's been challenging to watch them take flight on their own: college, engagements, new jobs, and new friends. A blessing, too, yes, but the reality of my "baby girls" not needing daddy so much is also heartbreaking.

The same is true with ministry. My pastor does not always have to call me, and I do not always have to call him, but it is good to know he is there should I need him. In some cases, the relationship with sons and daughters is daily, weekly, monthly—maybe yearly. The relationship often depends on need. But that son or daughter must know his or her parent in ministry is always available, willing to lift, model, and teach what it means to serve in this culture. I think that relationship is exactly what Drs. Crouch and Gregory have observed.

RESPONSE FROM REV. JINI KILGORE

Dr. Gregory and Dr. Crouch have captured some of the key features of mentoring upcoming pastors and ministers in the black church; however, their examples are mostly of sons in the ministry. I speak as a daughter in ministry and as one who has been mentored not only by a male senior pastor, who considers me to be his daughter in the ministry, but also by the "mothers" in the church, who played a significant role in my ministerial formation.

At the Second Baptist Church of Los Angeles, "Mother" Dolores Nehemiah, a former president of the Women's Auxiliary of the Progressive National Baptist Convention, spoke to me about proper pulpit attire and other matters when I became a minister. She and other church mothers were the precursors to women in ministry. Though their ministries predate the ordaining of women in the black Baptist church, as speakers in churches—usually for the annual Women's Day or Mission Sunday—they preached the Word.

Back in the day, a female speaker for Women's Day was often called a "preacher," speaking the anointed Word of God, and thus unknowingly serving as a mentor for the women of my generation who were the first in the black Baptist church to become licensed and ordained preachers. These mentors are not to be forgotten.

I began in this same tradition as a speaker for Women's Day. However, having come on the scene in the late seventies, at the opportune time for women, my speeches were called *sermons* by some who heard them, which helped me to acknowledge my calling as a gospel preacher. I am certain that women such as Dr. Nehemiah would have become preachers, likewise, had the opportunity been present as it was for my contemporaries and me.

Because some of these church mothers were preaching and ministering informally in many other ways (counseling, interceding in prayer, visiting the sick, administering programs, raising money, etc.), they have been the mentors, along with male pastors, of women—and even men—in ministry.

I am reminded of the late Mary Morris, a dynamic teacher of young adult Sunday school at Allen Temple Baptist Church, for whom an entire section of the church is now named. Many—if not most—of the young ministers at Allen Temple heard their calling during her tenure and under her tutelage. Her teaching style was definitely that of proclamation. She inspired hundreds of young adults to pick up some mantle of service in the church.

As church auxiliary leaders, particularly as heads of the traditional Women's Missionary Society, these women have led the way in shaping the church's mission programs and have been role models and mentors for the women coming up behind them. Much of their demeanor and style is evident in today's daughters in ministry. As a daughter in Christian ministry, I still speak in traditional black Baptist churches on Women's Day and wear the designated color of the day—usually white—along with a hat.

I could wear clergy attire, but to pay respects to my church mothers and role models, I choose to wear what the other women are wearing. I do it to signify that, long before anyone dared call me a preacher, many women were preaching in their white suits and hats. I also do so to say that a woman can be a woman, keeping a female persona, and still be a preacher. God calls men and women. God does not require that women imitate men. We do not have to adopt male models in dress or speech in order to preach the gospel. As Shakespeare's *Romeo and Juliet* declared, "A rose by any other name would smell as sweet."

Having said that, I am profoundly moved by Dr. Gregory's having caught the spirit of the mentor-mentee relationship in the black church. He is right about the ongoing bond between fathers and sons in the ministry, and he is keenly insightful pertaining to the Monday morning and Sunday evening recapitulation of the church service that goes on among pastors and their offspring in ministry across the length and breadth of this country. This type of togetherness is, indeed, a lifestyle.

My father in the ministry is Rev. Dr. J. Alfred Smith Sr., pastor emeritus of the Allen Temple Baptist Church in Oakland, California. Pastor Smith, as I refer to him, saw the calling in me before I acknowledged it. He encouraged and nurtured that calling, often giving me books to read from his voluminous library to challenge my thinking and my growth. Once I had accepted my calling to the Christian ministry, he welcomed me to the ministry-in-training program at Allen Temple, a structured program of apprenticeship in ministry. I also learned a lot about ministry from observing my natural father, the late Rev. Dr. Thomas Kilgore Jr., the first African American president of American Baptist Churches USA, a founder and president of the Progressive National Baptist Convention, and pastor of five churches during his lifetime, including the Second Baptist Church of Los Angeles. My calling in ministry convinced my father that women could be ministers as well as men. I was privileged to serve under his leadership in a well-structured ministry-in-training program at Second Baptist Church for a year before he retired from being the senior pastor there.

I equally appreciate Dr. Crouch's case studies of individual sons and pastors in ministry. I am reminded of Rev. Dr. Marcus D. Cosby, who sat for six years as an understudy of Dr. William Lawson at Wheeler Avenue Baptist Church in Houston, Texas, before becoming the church's new senior pastor. He learned well from his mentor, received the commendation of the church, and has taken the church to higher heights, while understanding the church's legacy and preserving its distinct identity.

This type of mentoring is becoming more evident as a natural way to pass on the baton when a senior pastor nears retirement. The same experience can be seen between biological father and son at Allen Temple Baptist Church in Oakland, California, where Rev. Dr. J. Alfred Smith Jr. served under his father for sixteen years before succeeding him as senior pastor. Rev. Otis Moss III served for two years as pastoral understudy to Rev. Dr. Jeremiah A. Wright Jr. at Trinity United Church of Christ in Chicago, Illinois, before succeeding him as pastor upon Dr. Wright's long-planned retirement.

This presents another very important aspect to mentorship, which the authors did not mention: mentorship can provide continuity of leadership and vision within a church congregation. This aspect is crucial because, all too often, a new pastor is not a good fit for a church congregation and brings disharmony between the "old" congregation and the "new" one. In a pastoral transition, when an incoming pastor changes or ignores the essential identity of the church, the old congregation experiences profound loss and grief. (Of course, the other side of this coin is that a church might need a change of direction that would best be served by someone new in its midst.)

The discussion between Dr. Gregory and Dr. Crouch has captured the spirit and practice of mentoring ministers, which is certainly one of the finer aspects of ministry in the black church.

RESPONSE FROM Rev. Bryan L. Carter

The experiences of Pastors Ashe, Leach, and Jemison are definitely indicative of the historic relationship between a pastor and a son in the ministry. The mentor-mentee relationship truly gives the inexperienced minister the affirmation, inspiration, and correction that he or she needs to have the foundational practices for ministry.

Dr. Crouch is right on target when he affirms that mentoring helps provide the bridge from the theoretical to daily practices. Mentoring affords one to be able to understand the practical implications of ministry, because the seminary experiences only provide brief exposure. Additionally, every minister may not have the opportunity to attend seminary, thus heightening the value and importance of mentoring.

The experience between pastor and son or pastor and daughter is so instrumental in development that those being mentored may not fully understand the importance until they become pastors. It is amazing how one assumes so much when watching from the outside, but when one has to sit in that pastoral seat, everything changes. Without the mentoring of a seasoned man or woman of God, it is extremely difficult to have sustained success in ministry.

My mentor and predecessor, the late Dr. E. K. Bailey, would paraphrase Proverbs 16:25 by saying, "Sometimes there is a way that seems to be right to the young preacher, but in the end it is the way to get put out." Mentoring is irreplaceable, and its value is seen throughout Scripture in the life of Moses and Joshua, Elijah and Elisha, Paul and Timothy, Jesus and his disciples.

As Dr. Gregory expressed, "We are in this together" is an accurate description of the network among black pastors and mentees. There is shared ownership in that those being mentored are proud to be associated with their mentor pastors, and the pastors deeply desire success for their children in the ministry. Both groups reap benefits from the shared lifetime bond. There is genuine interest and a reciprocal relationship that takes place. When I was successful, Dr. Bailey would share his pride. He desired for me to stand on his shoulders, because he once stood on the shoulders of men who came before him.

I was deeply humbled to even be associated with him, and he took great joy in encouraging and guiding me. Dr. Bailey mentored twelve preachers, including me, through weekly teachings on Saturday morning for an entire year. He shared life principles and best practices for ministry, and he challenged us in life's every arena. The value of mentorship cannot be understated, and I know from personal experience that it is an integral aspect of the African American church community.

✣ Takeaways

1. Invest time and energy in the life of another potential pastor who feels the weight and blessing of God's call on his or her life.

2. Make a commitment to be a mentor. Not only will you grow spiritually, you will enhance someone else's journey and create a lifetime relationship that benefits you both.

3. Be accountable to another pastor in your ministry. Find someone with whom you can confide, connect, and be yourself.

4. The nature of the pastorate can be lonely; make a commitment to move past your comfort zone and allow yourself to be ministered to.

Note

1. "Blessed Be the Tie That Binds," words by John Fawcett, 1782.

CHAPTER 5

FREEDOM OF EXPRESSION

*Now the Lord is the Spirit, and where the Spirit
of the Lord is, there is freedom. (2 Corinthians 3:17)*

JOEL'S REFLECTION

Freedom in worship and to worship may be one of *the* hallmarks
of the black church experience. The sense of freedom evidences
itself from the first moments of the service to the concluding
benediction. That freedom can be found in the liturgy, in the
music, and in the message. In contrast, traditionally in white culture (although not always), a hymn or praise song may be sung
only for a specific amount of time. When the song is over, worship is *over*. In other words, when all four stanzas have been
sung or the chorus has been repeated a final time, the worship
experience is complete.

Not so in the black church. My experience has shown me the
stirring and unscripted power of a hymn, anthem, or praise song
as this mysterious thing. The Holy Spirit moves throughout the
congregation, and members remain in that moment—singing. In
a gradual crescendo of praise, the words or phrases are sung
again and again, embedding the message into the collective psy-
che of the congregation. There appears to be no pressure, no
feeling of being haunted by the clock, no external drive to move
toward the next item in the order of worship. The congregation

stays in that moment of praise until its collective consciousness shifts to the next movement of the Spirit.

But African American worship services are not simply free flowing with little theological or liturgical structure. It has been my experience that even in black churches where no formal order of worship exists; the leadership invests great spiritual consideration in the development of a service. Time is made for the Spirit to do what the Spirit does. The same is true with the preached Word. When the minister reaches a thought or a lived experience that strikes fire within the congregation, the preacher stays with that thought. And congregants may respond by saying to the preacher, "Stay right there."

These responses from the pew are welcome feedback for the minister to explore more fully and passionately the movement of the sermon. The freedom of the congregation and the preacher in this call-and-response dynamic makes black preaching a communal experience that is proclaimed not only *to* the people but also *with* the people.

BILL'S REFLECTION

I am about as Baptist as one could possibly be. I was born in a Baptist hospital and into a second-generation-Baptist-pastor's home. At age ten, I was the state Bible-verse champion at the Baptist Assembly. I attended Baptist summer camps, and I am a graduate of two Baptist colleges and hold two degrees from a Baptist seminary. I have been a patient at a Baptist hospital and an employee of a Baptist children's home and of three Baptist colleges. So, I guess I'm destined to live in a Baptist retirement home and bound to be buried in a Baptist cemetery. The point is, I know Baptist people.

Unfortunately, those experiences were not diverse; they were solely with white Baptists. And I have found that white Baptists often criticize those who praise the Lord out loud in church, sway to the music, raise their hands in praise, or talk to the preacher during the sermon. When I reflect, I don't remember much joy in my worship experience, and there was certainly little freedom of expression.

Now, five years into my journey with black men and women of God, I have found a freedom in worship I have never before experienced. I have found a rhythm in the dancing words, swaying feet, raised hands, and singing preachers, and in an engaged and connected congregation praying and praising together. There is joy in the worship, unspeakable joy.

JOEL'S REFLECTION

In the black church experience, freedom of expression takes on many forms. In both the musical worship and the proclamation of the Word, worshippers respond in various ways. With the praise music, some people remain seated, while others stand. Some sway, and others raise hands. Some clap; others dance with praise. There appears to be no stifling sense of conformity, and there certainly appears to be little stigma attached to a given response during praise and worship. Worship in the black church is a celebration of God's gifts and the Lord's goodness.

This freedom of expression goes to the heart of the Bible. David danced before the Lord. That is fact, fundamental and biblical. To this day, Orthodox Jews pray while swaying back and forth, to demonstrate their love for God.

Freedom of expression also extends to the time of the invitation. In black church culture, the invitation to accept Christ is typically an appeal by the pastor, but it can also become a congregational and collective experience. The preacher may exhort the congregation, "Turn to the person next to you. Ask him if he knows the Lord and has a church home." Dr. Ralph D. West Sr. often follows this with, "Tell the person next to you that you cannot walk for her, but you will walk with her."

This word of encouragement is remarkably effective in motivating people to make a spiritual decision. It is neither in perception nor reality manipulative or coercive. It is expected, desired, and effective. In contrast, people in other cultures can be sensitive to the mildest request to join the body of Christ. Nevertheless, there is a legitimate place for spiritual persuasion through human instrumentality.

My paternal grandmother, Lena Hornback, represented an early era in Texas Baptist life. During my boyhood, she recalled scenes from the early twentieth century when white Baptist farmwomen would shout and dance before the Lord under outdoor brush arbors in West Texas when their children or husbands were converted to the Christian faith. These were otherwise simple women, quiet in demeanor and extremely self-possessed. Those expressions might now be discounted as aberrations or relics of an uninformed era.

Many subtle cultural reasons contribute to the reticence of white folks today to express ourselves openly during worship, but I remain hopeful that the white church culture is moving toward more freedom and spontaneity in worship. Surely we can recover some of that Spirit-filled emotion and passion in church culture across the board.

BILL'S REFLECTION

It was the first Sunday of the month, and I was visiting St. John Church in Grand Prairie, Texas. The pastor, Rev. Denny D. Davis, invited me to sit on the dais with him. The first Sunday in many black churches is Communion Sunday, but I was totally unprepared for what I was about to experience. The pastor came into the pulpit before the meditation hymn and asked for all who had birthdays that month to stand up. It just happened to be my birthday, so I joined the twenty or so people who rose to their feet.

I noticed the congregation's pleasure as the keyboardist began to play "Happy Birthday." A few measures into the music, the keyboardist stopped, and the congregation began to clap as the pastor, a big man with a deep voice, began to sing the birthday song in a way I had never heard. He waved his arms, building up to a climax, and held the next-to-last note for about fifteen seconds. Then he hit the highest note I have ever heard a big man produce. For me, it was quite a moment!

Church members rose to their feet and shouted. The pastor had related to the congregation in a way few would have attempted. Birthday folks had been honored, while others in the congregation had been pleasantly entertained. I laughed, but then it hit me. What Pastor Davis had just done was to say to his people, "I love you so much that we can have fun, joke, and be vulnerable while experiencing all God has given us in the body of Christ." It might not have seemed that way to anyone else, but I sat down feeling I had just participated in a powerfully expressive moment of communication.

RESPONSE FROM Rev. JACQUELINE A. THOMPSON

Drs. Crouch and Gregory offer the reader a unique, bird's-eye view into the Sunday morning worship experience of many black churches throughout the country. Whether in song, the preached word, the period of giving, the invitation to discipleship, or even the style of dress, there is a treasured freedom of expression worthy of reflection and analysis.

But inherent in their observation is also an irony worthy of analysis as well: The freedom of expression in worship described as one of the "hallmarks of the black church experience" by Dr. Gregory was birthed during a tortured time in history when blacks definitely were not allowed to express themselves and certainly were not free.

Like the present-day black church, its predecessor, the invisible slave church, was a place where freedom of expression was paramount. Slaves would gather in worship and engage in rituals all expressing the joy of freedom—not a physical freedom, but a spiritual freedom. The singing, dancing, shouting, clapping, and testifying were reflective of the liberation of the spirit and soul. Slaves would leave these gatherings empowered spiritually, enabled to persevere and endure dehumanizing conditions until divine physical deliverance came.

The historical reality suggests that physical expression in the black church conveys the joy of freedom but is also reflective of the power in the freedom of expression itself. The freedom of expression in worship has the power to transform, revive, renew, restore, strengthen, and empower, all while imparting joy, hope, and peace to the lives of those worshipping.

This power is transcendent in nature, moving beyond the limits of race, class, culture, and religious denomination and going to the heart of our faith. I suggest it may even go straight to the heart of God—the same God who delivers us from bondage so we might be free to come together as one people, God's people, and express ourselves in worship. This is the common ground we all stand on as Christians.

> For in Christ Jesus you are all children of God through faith. As many of you as were baptized into Christ have clothed yourselves with Christ. There is no longer Jew or Greek, there is no longer slave or free, there is no longer male and female; for all of you are one in Christ Jesus. And if you belong to Christ, then you are Abraham's offspring, heirs according to the promise. (Galatians 3:26-29)

Now that's a freedom we can all celebrate.

The authors suggest that freedom of expression in the black church offers many lessons that might enhance the worship and spirituality of its white counterparts. However, comparable lessons pose a challenge for the black church as she moves into the future. The black church must guard against becoming the oppressor of the next generations. She must work diligently to ensure that the freedom of expression, which has been born out of oppression and come to characterize the worship experience, does not cause her to become the oppressor in an effort to preserve that experience.

Many churches across racial and denominational lines struggle to remain relevant to their young people. Key to maintaining a meaningful connection with this population is allowing a worship experience that speaks to that generation. The shift to contemporary gospel music, the introduction of praise and worship teams, and the incorporation of the liturgical arts are all modes of expression that enhance the spirituality and worship experience of this generation. But these changes occasionally meet with resistance in some traditional black church settings. We who are older sometimes forget that Jesus met people where they were—by speaking their language, using analogies from their daily lives, and visiting them where they lived. We ought to be doing the same in this generation.

There are lessons here to be learned by all people, black and white and of every other culture and race. The apostle Paul articulates it best: "For freedom Christ has set us free. Stand firm, therefore, and do not submit again to a yoke of slavery" (Galatians 5:1).

RESPONSE FROM **REV. DR. A. LOUIS PATTERSON JR.**

This reflective commentary by Drs. Gregory and Crouch brings into focus the importance to those in the African American church tradition of free expression, which results in an extended channel of glory to God.

Drs. Crouch and Gregory accurately highlight freedom of expression as one element in the order and occasion of our worship. The freedom of expression in the black church may be historically analogous to several biblical incidents. Remember the leper as recorded in Luke 17:15, "Then one of them, when he saw that he was healed, turned back, praising God with a loud voice." Remember the man at the gate Beautiful in Acts 3, or the man at the pool in John 5. The end result will usually express itself in walking, leaping, and praising God.

As with these people featured in biblical narrative, African Americans have been an oppressed people but a people who survived, thrived, and endured. Whenever a people are confined and shackled but survive to be set free, there is an efficacious expression of energy demonstrated mentally, emotionally, and physically.

In the black church, celebration is associated with the musical presentation, the preached Word, the call and response, and the spiritual ebb and flow of worship. Emancipation—freedom—is associated with the proclamation of the gospel. It involves a demonstration associated with having been delivered from that which Congress could no longer legislate, presidents could no longer veto, penal systems could no longer confine, and courts could no longer adjudicate, because it was divine deliverance, development, and destiny. As in our culture historically, having been delivered, we freely express ourselves. So it is in our spiritual relationship with Christ.

We "were dead through the trespasses and sins, . . . but God, who is rich in mercy, . . . made us alive together with Christ . . . and raised us up with him" (Ephesians 2:1, 4-6). Therefore, we enter into the worship experience where, through Christ, in Christ, with Christ, for Christ, unto Christ, and on our way to being like Christ, all debts have been cancelled and erased from the books. All criminal charges have been dropped with records expunged. There are real and abundant reasons to be like our brother David and make a joyful noise, expressing our love for God. We, as God's people, black, white, red, or brown, should shout and show ourselves *alive!*

❄ TAKEAWAYS

1. Exercise freedom in your worship by varying the order of service. This might involve rearranging the order of service elements or adding a new element, such as a different musical style or a performance ministry such as drama, dance, or mime.

2. Allow new voices—or silences—in your worship service. Invite congregational response, or introduce a period of meditation where no voices at all are heard.

3. Consider what it would look like for your congregation to exercise greater freedom of expression in worship. Would you risk "staying there" by repeating a stanza in song or by extrapolating from your sermon manuscript when you sense a connection with the congregation? What about closing your eyes, clapping with the music, raising your hands, or inviting the congregation to talk back to you as the preacher?

CHAPTER 6

STURDY BRIDGES:
HONORING ELDERS

Do not speak harshly to an older man,
but speak to him as to a father . . .
to older women as mothers. . . . (1 Timothy 5:1-2)

BILL'S REFLECTION

One of my most significant discoveries about the black men and women of God has been their enormous respect for elders. Evidence of respect can be seen all around the black church. It can be seen in the way the pastors treat more seasoned ministers and congregants. It can be seen in the time taken during worship to recognize the "mother" of the church. It is demonstrated in sermons when the pastor pauses reflectively and says, "as the old folks say," or "as my grandmother used to say." There is weight given to the words and honor to the actions of the older members of the congregation.

These are not merely transitional phrases or sermonic devices used to get from one point to the next. When respect for elders is shown in a sermon, the congregation gives a vocal response. Someone else's grandmother hummed the same hymn while cooking. Someone else's grandfather told similar stories of T. E. "Bull" Connor's dogs and "whites only" water fountains. In other words, the effect is relational. The elders have amassed great wisdom about living and overcoming, regardless of their education or societal station. There is much to be learned from those who have endured and have survived.

Age is equated with wisdom, and the black men and women of God listen to the experiences and knowledge of those who came before them. Extraordinary efforts are made to accommodate elders of the church. Honor is bestowed on them, often in special recognition times during the services. When an older minister stands behind the pulpit, there is a level of respect granted to him or her that is unlike what I have seen in the white community, with the exception of Rev. Dr. Billy Graham.

I witnessed this respect for elders when I attended a gathering of Bishop College ministerial alumni. It was a reunion of sorts, as well as a time for discussion about the alumni's futures, and I was invited to present a proposal about a possible relationship between Georgetown College and Bishop College.

After the working session, we gathered for lunch and a sermon by a retired professor and administrator whom they all loved, Rev. Dr. Harry S. Wright. Dr. Wright had been retired for many years and was living in South Carolina. Many had not seen him for some time. As Dr. Wright stood to speak, a hush fell over the luncheon crowd. For the next thirty minutes, all of us were mesmerized by the soft but brilliant insights he shared about Judas, "the disciple who almost made it."

By the end of his sermon, all of us were standing as Dr. Wright concluded his remarks. (In the African American church, standing during a sermon is a compliment the hearer gives the preacher. It is an indication of support and that the preacher is on the right track.) I was greatly affected by his sermon, but as I stood there, I was also thinking about how few times in my culture that elderly men and women of God are invited into gatherings to share a word from the Lord.

There is much to be learned, and I can't help feeling that blessings are being missed when we fail to honor our elders in the faith and in ministry.

JOEL'S REFLECTION

Often, in my experience, when black pastors gather for coffee and conversation, talk invariably turns to tales of legendary ministers, the great elders among African American preachers still living, including Rev. Dr. Gardner C. Taylor, Rev. Dr. Caesar Clark, Rev. Dr. Charles G. Adams, Rev. Dr. William J. Shaw, Rev. Dr. Wyatt Tee Walker, Rev. Dr. Harry Wright, Rev. Dr. Otis Moss Jr., and Rev. Dr. James A. Forbes Jr., just to name a few, because the list truly could go on. Then, the talk turns to those legends who are now with the ancestors of our faith: Rev. Dr. E. K. Bailey, Rev. Dr. Sandy Ray, Rev. Dr. Thomas Kilgore Jr., Rev. Dr. Samuel DeWitt Proctor, Rev. Dr. William Augustus Jones Jr., Rev. Dr. Manuel Scott Sr., and Rev. Dr. Kelly Miller Smith Sr. And this list, too, could go on and on.

Late into the night, stories of preaching, pastoring, convention leadership, and personalities fill the room and the conversation. For instance, many varied stories are told of Rev. Dr. J. H. Jackson, who was president of the National Baptist Convention USA, from his battles with Martin Luther King Jr. and Gardner Taylor to his pulpit oratory and powerful leadership. All the stories are incredibly intriguing. I have heard eyewitnesses describe how, before the NBCUSA controversial 1961 presidential election, Jackson's powerful preaching had even some of his opponents shouting encouragement.

The constellation of elders is like an unseen cloud of witnesses when preachers gather to discuss their lives and ministries. The elders' presence is tangible, palpable. Old stories are recounted and new anecdotes added as the lives of the elders are rehearsed and etched into memory. Their sermons are abridged and repeated, their ministerial foibles and strengths noted, and their longevity praised.

For example, I have been involved with Bill in the renewal efforts of Bishop College through the Bishop College Alive Project at Georgetown College, Kentucky. The names of Drs. Harry S. Wright, John D. Mangrum, L. K. Williams, and Richard

Rollins, revered elders of Bishop, constantly occupy alumni conversations. These men are so respected, and though their shadows are lengthened, their influence does not wane, so mentoring continues. While I use Bishop as an example, I know the experience repeats itself for those from other historically black institutions like Morehouse College, Virginia Union, Fisk, Howard, and Hampton Universities, for legendary African American preachers graduated from those schools as well.

Perhaps few things in black ministerial life stand in starker contrast with white ministerial life than this awareness of how one generation stands on the shoulders of its elders and ancestors. With some notable exceptions, I perceive that younger white preachers live in a historical vacuum concerning preachers of older generations. The iconic names of thirty years ago are soon forgotten. The interest is often centered on the latest phenomenon in the post-modern church. Most are concerned with the twenty-something-who-is-packing-them-in mentality.

Dr. John Albert Broadus, one of the first professors at the Southern Baptist Theological Seminary and author of one of the most famous textbooks on preaching in American history, *On the Preparation and Delivery of Sermons* (1870); Rev. George W. Truett, pastor of First Baptist Church, Dallas, Texas, past president of the Southern Baptist Convention and of the Baptist World Alliance; legendary evangelist Rev. Dr. Vance H. Havner (Bill's great-uncle); Rev. Dr. Theodore Adams, former president of the Baptist World Alliance; Rev. Dr. Edward Hughes Pruden, who gave one of the inaugural invocations for President Harry S. Truman's second inauguration; and Rev. J. D. Gray, pastor of First Baptist Church, New Orleans, Louisiana, and past president of the Southern Baptist Convention, are just a few names lost on the present generation of white preachers. The preaching of the gospel did not just begin in earnest with this generation, no matter what our race or culture.

We all stand on the shoulders of those whose names and ministries should be remembered. The black preacher senses this "romance of the pulpit," to borrow a phrase. So when a black proclaimer stands, a cloud of unseen witnesses surrounds him or her in the preaching moment. Preaching with amnesia about our predecessors can create arrogance on the one hand and discouragement on the other. We did not invent preaching, nor are we the first to have trials in it. We should honor those who paved the way (many of whom suffered indignities so the next generation would not have to)—honor them, praise them, and call them blessed, but most of all remember.

BILL'S REFLECTION

For the past three years, I have attended the E. K. Bailey International Expository Preaching Conference in Dallas, Texas. I went to continue developing my network among black preachers and to lead a class this past year on fundraising in the local church. For me, the highlight of the conference has been the Living Legends Luncheon. This was started by Dr. Bailey to honor seniors in ministry who have set an example, have opened doors, and have modeled preaching at its best.

At least one thousand people fill the International Ballroom at the Fairmont Hotel for the luncheon. As one enters, there are large pictures of each legend who has been previously honored. The luncheon begins with a march of former honorees, followed by the new honoree, all walking on a red carpet runner. All in attendance rise to recognize these outstanding ministers.

The luncheon is always an elegant affair, with linen tablecloths and, honestly, the best banquet food one could wish for. The musicians uplift the crowd's spirits. The program is well orchestrated, and the focus is on the senior honoree. Wonderful testimonies are shared, and when the honoree takes the podium, it is to a hero's welcome. Then the legend almost always speaks about the great men and women of God who laid the groundwork for his or her ministry, and the names are called as if in a prayerful litany.

Even though I have known none of the honorees personally, I am always moved to tears by the significance of the moment. I confess I am also overcome with a bit of guilt because I know

I have neglected to thank preachers and others who have made a difference in my ministry. I have determined to rectify this and have started by establishing a relationship with a former Hebrew and Old Testament professor, Dr. John I. Durham. Together we have designed a program of fellowship for 25 ministers with a focus on celebration and joy. This will be the third conclave we have administered together. Dr. Durham and I have now established a rich bond, much like a father and son.

JOEL'S REFLECTION

A touching aspect of the black church is the special veneration saved for the mothers of the church. These are faithful, dedicated women who have served long and well, and in the autumn of their lives enjoy recognition and respect. In many churches the mothers occupy special seats, and in nearly all churches, they receive special recognition.

On one particular Sunday at Greater New Bethel Baptist, the church of Rev. Dr. Earl A. Pleasant in Inglewood, California, some of the mothers got an honor I'm not sure they anticipated. The church celebrated its anniversary by dividing into three stewardship teams, each competing with the other to give gifts for the anniversary.

Each team danced and celebrated down the center aisle and around the sanctuary in a rousing moment of joy and giving. At the end of this procession, dancing attendants energetically whirled the mothers of the church around in their wheelchairs, and the venerated senior ladies became the delighted objects of everyone's attention.

The church loved it, the senior ladies rejoiced and laughed, and the pastor beamed from the pulpit. The congregation's desire to honor their elders created a moment of praise coupled with much joy. These ladies had no sense of being marginalized, sidelined, or superannuated.

Rev. Dr. Joe Carter of New Hope Missionary Baptist Church in Newark, New Jersey, seats the mothers in his church in special pews perpendicular to the congregation. At the beginning of every service, he stops to hug and greet them. Their wisdom is recognized, their experience valued, and their self-esteem affirmed. In a culture intoxicated with youth and the present, this is a visible reminder to the entire congregation about the value of their elder members. The elders are a visual and tangible definition of respect, and it is a blessing young people can witness Sunday after Sunday.

RESPONSE FROM REV. DR. SUSAN K. WILLIAMS SMITH

For black church people, none are quite so precious to us as the elders. It is they who have weathered the storms of racism, bad education, and unjust judicial systems, and who prove daily by their presence that "God is good—all the time."

I will never forget an old woman who came to a prayer meeting at Bethel AME Church in Baltimore, Maryland, some years ago. She was old, with deep-set eyes and cheeks sunken, largely, because she had no teeth. Her face looked leathery, and her wrinkles had to have been etched upon her face. When it was time for the testimony service, she stood up. It was as though she had the light of God shining directly on her, and that light seemed to grow brighter with her words.

"I lost ev'erthing I ever had today," she said. "There was a fire in my house. I been in that house goin' on fifty years. Raised my chiren there. Lost ev'rthing." I remember holding my breath. "But I'm here to tell you," she said, "that I ain't never seen the righteous forsaken. I loves my God. I loves my God, and ain't no fire gwine change that. I ain't got my house, but I got Jesus!"

The church went up in praise. The old woman stood there, resolute, proud, and sure of her God. Her story and strength clearly represent the power of elders, who pushed through tragedy and whose lives remind us of what really matters.

Bill Crouch is right when he observes that black preachers give weighty respect to the presence and power of our elders. There *is* weight in what they say. The elders remind us that, because of God, we made it through the rough waters of hatred and discrimination. They remind us that with God, all things are possible. Their presence and testimonies often energize the faithful for the road ahead. In fact, that is exactly what their testimonies *have* done.

The power of the black preacher is legendary. It is not surprising that a hush falls over the room when revered, old black preachers enter. They had the resolve, the faith, and the passion to keep a people afloat when times were heinously hard. They brought people to tears, tears that cleaned out pain and fear and anxiety, and gave church members the "food" needed to survive a hostile world.

The elder preachers took the stories of the biblical heroes and brought their experiences down to the ghettos and neighborhoods, convincing and convicting people that God could and would make all things bearable.

The connectedness between the elders and younger folks is a gem. For this writer, hearing someone like Rev. Dr. Jeremiah A. Wright Jr. basting the harsh experiences of racism with the butter of sure faith made those experiences palatable. Black preachers like Bishop John Richard Bryant and Dr. Wright never allowed young people to even entertain that giving up was an option. The elders had the responsibility to teach that God is good and to teach *why* they said God is good. Whatever happened, we were *not* to give in or give up. This God was the same God who had walked with Moses and the Israelites through the wilderness. They preached that God had done it before, that God would do it again and, in fact, that God was doing it even now in the present.

It is indeed sad if this connectedness is not a part of the white preaching experience. For black people, the blessed assurance was presented to us in the flesh through the presence and power of black preachers and the preaching of our elders. Their words were able to make Jesus accessible to us, which was a gift since so much was not accessible. The preaching of the preachers and the testimonies of the revered made us know we were worth something to God. Surely, the mother of the church would remind us in bad times that there was nothing God could not do. The mother could rock anxious souls to a spiritual peace with recollections of how God could do everything but fail.

I remember when Rev. Dr. Prathia Hall Wynn, now deceased, had been invited to Trinity United Church of Christ in Chicago, Illinois, for Women's Day. She was late getting in, and we were on notice that someone might have to "be ye also ready." But midway through the service, she came in, and she preached with a power I cannot explain on paper. Afterward, she said she was late because her daughter, who had given birth the day before, had fallen into a coma and suffered a stroke.

I was amazed. Dr. Wynn had not said a word about her personal dilemma in her sermon. When I looked at her, my eyes asking why and how, she smiled. "God is taking care of her," she said. "When God takes care of someone, you don't have to worry. God told me to come on here, so I did."

The lesson has never left me. Dr. Wynn showed the peculiar and amazing strength of elders in the black church. I cannot imagine a world or a church without elders, those who have passed as well as those still living. The words of Gardner Taylor, Ella and Henry Mitchell, Samuel B. McKinney, Prathia Hall Wynn, William Augustus Jones, Jeremiah A Wright Jr., and Bishop John Richard Bryant have been spiritual food for so many seeking God.

It is an honor to reach elder status. Being recognized as an elder means you know God never fails. That the honor given to elders was not lost on Joel Gregory and Bill Crouch and is a testimony to this reality in the black church, a reality that has to be considered a gift from God to us.

RESPONSE FROM REV. DR. IVAN DOUGLAS HICKS

I, too, celebrate the gifts of our elders. They are to be revered, for they can inspire us to greatness. Most of us have to admit, especially during these exciting but troubled times, that life can be a challenge. Yet, the elder deacons, missionaries, church mothers, and stewards inspire in those who hear their stories and testimonies a desire to keep on keeping on.

Through our more seasoned parishioners, young people are able to see real-time examples of Christian maturity. Exposure to our elders' examples helps develop new Christians, and our elders' stories of spiritual success in battles fought and trials endured is incredibly inspirational.

One must understand the African American church community to appreciate our devotion to our elders. Historically, the church has been a place where honor could be bestowed. The church has also purposefully fostered leadership among men, who have too often remained unplaced and unsupported in wider society. So the African American church has provided leadership opportunities, ranking, position, and even titles for those men who have been faithful to their churches and to their God.

Bill and Joel noted earlier that one of the greatest tributes given to an African American preacher is to stand as he or she concludes or comes to a salient point in the sermon. But even more than responsive crowds, standing listeners, and well-timed and well-pitched music—much more profound, in my estimation—is what Hebrews 12:1 describes as a host of witnesses, the elders and those who have gone on, who cheer us as we run the race for God's glory.

Not only do ministers believe that the preaching moment is touched by heaven, but true believers understand and enter the sanctuary expecting an encounter with the holy. If God, Jesus, the Holy Ghost, Moses, and varied configurations of angels can be met in worship, then the spirits of our mothers and fathers can be found there, also.

If you ever want to get a response in an African American worship service, just ask the congregation if they can appreciate and praise God for a praying mother—an elder. Ask if they can praise God because somebody took the time to pray for them. You will strike a nerve, triggering a resounding and collective yes.

We place high value on remembering those who have made a difference in our churches, our communities, and our lives. Some will even say that the spirit of one who has gone on now rests on another who fills the role of the departed—even as Elisha sought the spiritual (and material) mantle of Elijah. Libations may be poured during cultural celebrations for those loved ones who are no longer with us. Church nurseries, fellowship halls, and senior centers may be named for longtime and committed church workers, or a particular program may be named in a spiritual hero's honor. Most congregations have an epic memory, so when prayers go forward and history is recounted, the names of those who have joined the ancestors are lifted.

It is a part of our church culture to remember to give flowers now, while our elders still live, when and where honor is due. We hold in great esteem our seasoned saints—our griots. For example, while serving as executive director of the Hampton Ministers' Conference, Rev. Dr. Timothy Tee Boddie edited a book of interviews of senior statesmen entitled *Wisdom of the Sages*.[1] Every year, Bishop J. Douglas Wiley hosts the Gardner Calvin Taylor Distinguished Preaching Series to honor the life, preaching, and ministry of his "father," Rev. Dr. Gardner C. Taylor, once heralded by *TIME* magazine as the Dean of the Nation's Black Preachers.

In many ways, the preaching and ministries of our older pastors are being preserved and published so that their rich oration and advice can be shared with emerging students of preaching. While my personal fear is that much of our great tradition will be lost, left only to gatherings where the topic is pursued, the legendary preachers of our tradition cannot be forgotten. We stand on their shoulders.

I have my own family as a handy illustration, but on my journey there have been great preacher-pastor friends and heroes of the church who have radically impacted my ministry, including Samuel DeWitt Proctor, Henry and Ella Pearson Mitchell, Prathia Hall Wynn, William Augustus Jones, and Marvis Proctor May.

When opportunity permits, I can be found sitting at a dining room table or in a restaurant after a worship service, and I often end up a blessed recipient of an oral history being passed down by our faith's elders, our griots, and the prophetic voices of God. I listen, and I learn, in an effort to be a better pastor. Poetically, and in many instances vicariously, these preachers are found transmitting the ethos, the culture, and even the aesthetic image of the African American preacher.

I have enjoyed the opportunity to sit with African American elders. I have heard familiar tales replete with both humor and passion. Preachers from Bishop College seek not only to employ, but also to embody the preaching of Dr. Manuel Scott and Dr. Harry S. Wright. Those who have matriculated at the Samuel DeWitt Proctor School of Theology at Virginia Union, like J. Weldon Gilbert, tell war stories of the teaching of the legendary Dr. Miles Jones and, more recently, of Dr. John W. Kinney. At most institutions where African American preachers gather, there are mentors who inspired those who would dare to be both curious students and clever practitioners of the unique craft of African American preaching.

Yes, programs honor the elderly, and elders are afforded a well-respected place in the life of the church, but there is something more mystical at play. The reality of our condition lends itself to close relationships with our elders until they die. But in the quest to understand the special appreciation we have for the elderly, don't fail to recognize that our respect for them is not until death, but is beyond death.

The names I lifted have been of important people who now happen to be in varied spiritual states. Our ancestors instruct and inspire us in the same way as those who are wise and very present do. Never forget there are those who are even older than the oldest member in our gatherings. And they cheer us on.

Cheering me are generations of prayers and practice. My calling is clear, so I am "wind assisted" by H. Beecher Hicks Jr., H. Beecher Hicks Sr., Theodore Roosevelt Harrison, William "Squire" Hicks, James Monroe Frazier, my mama, her ma dear, and everybody's big mama.

I affirm Crouch and Gregory's keen observations, but the challenge remains to understand the nature of the oldest presence in the rooms of our life and ministry. Perhaps a growing awareness of that cloud of witnesses will help us in our preaching and in the very way we dispense ministry—that we will be ever mindful of those who urge us on as we run this race.

✳ TAKEAWAYS

1. Create a church culture that recognizes the continuity of the Christian faith. We indeed stand on the shoulders of others.

2. Make special places and occasions to recognize the oldest members of the church. Do not marginalize, but validate them as heroes of the faith.

3. Create opportunities for the youth of the church to be actively involved in seniors' lives, so a culture of respect for the elderly can be built.

NOTES

1. Timothy Tee Boddie, ed. *Wisdom of the Sages: Conversations with the A. C. D. Vaughn Senior Statesmen, 1996–2005 Hampton University Ministers' Conference* (Chicago: Urban Ministries, Inc., 2007).

CHAPTER 7

THE POWER OF TOUCH

A time to embrace. . . . (Ecclesiastes 3:5)

BILL'S REFLECTION

On a summer Sunday morning, I was a visitor at a large, white Baptist church. The parking lot was nearly full, and all indications told me this was a happening place. Entering the closest building off the parking lot, I was welcomed to church by an official greeter with a friendly smile, a nametag in place, and a nice solid handshake. I truly anticipated a good experience.

Two hours later, I left the church with a somewhat different feeling. The church music had been uplifting. The sermon was inspiring. Nevertheless, between the opening handshakes from the official greeter and the courteous handshake from the church's pastor as I left the service, I felt isolated.

Even though a few nods from fellow worshippers, a pleasant smile from the usher, and a request from the pulpit to fill out a visitor card were all well-intentioned, the acts instead gave me an overwhelming feeling of being an outside observer to a religious ritual rather than a welcomed participant.

Contrast that Sunday with my experience at New Covenant Missionary Baptist Church, a large African American church in Chicago, Illinois. Again, I was visiting, and again, a welcoming host greeted me, but that is where the similarities between the two churches ceased.

The greetings at New Covenant were decidedly different. Yes, a handshake took place, but this greeting was just a tad more involved, and it felt much more personal. Let me explain. For lack of a proper title or name, let's just call the greeting the *lean*. The lean is where right hands grip in a traditional handshake, but left hands wrap around the other's back and right shoulders lean in and touch. I now understand it to be a nearly universal salutation among African American men. But this Sunday morning, for me, it felt special and inclusive. It felt like acceptance.

But that was just the beginning.

The greeter didn't just offer a generic welcome, but asked my name and occupation. Upon learning that I was a visiting clergyman, the greeter insisted on escorting me to the pastor's office. There, I was introduced to the pastor, the assistant pastor, and the senior deacon—and treated to the lean by all present. As a visiting Baptist minister, I was asked by New Covenant's pastor, Rev. Dr. Stephen J. Thurston Sr., to remain with him in his office while the choir director led the congregation in preworship praise and singing. Then I accompanied Dr. Thurston into the sanctuary where I was to sit with him at the pulpit.

As we walked in, every deacon I encountered gave me the lean. They did not know my name, but I was with their pastor, so I received the recognition of brotherhood. I know that it may seem in some ways naïve, but I was amazed. The service had just begun, and I was already a part of the fellowship. I felt alive in the Lord. And putting aside the public recognition and esteem for my clergy status, my sense of welcome and fellowship was in large part because of the power of touch!

JOEL'S REFLECTION

The lean, as Bill explained, is a tactile expression of welcome, brotherhood, and acceptance in the black community. Some realities cannot be articulated in words. If those realities could be expressed verbally, one would not need a physical expression like the lean. The dance pioneer Isadora Duncan was once asked what was meant by a particular dance. She responded, "If I could tell you what it meant, there would be no point in dancing it." So it is with the lean.

And while this greeting may not have direct theological implications, it has had incredible significance for us, two white theologians becoming part of the world of the African American church. The power of touch and the physical connection we have felt in African American churches and worship services throughout the country have been moving and instructive experiences. The power of touch alters the tone and tenor of worship and creates a distinct connection between members of the body of Christ.

Another kind of touch in black churches is what I would call *confrontive*. Now, I do not use *confrontive* to mean confrontational in a hostile sense. Rather, in the African American church experience, I have witnessed confrontive touch happening during service and often during the preaching moment. The confrontive touch involves a spiritual question or warm word of affirmation directed toward the person sitting closest to you. The preacher may do call for this confrontive interaction in order to engage the congregation and to help them to become active listeners and participants in the service. But the effect is the same.

It works like this: The preacher may say, "Turn to the person on your right, take his or her hand, and ask, 'Has God blessed you in a special way today?'" The congregants, mostly without self-consciousness and in a way that does not patronize others, do exactly that. A quiet but respectful buzz prevails while these exchanges take place. And then the preaching continues.

A variation of the confrontive touch may take place during the public invitation to accept Christ, join the church, and respond to the preaching of the gospel. Some pastors say, "Touch your neighbor and say, 'I cannot walk for you, but I will walk with you.'" This affirmation and support can have a powerful effect. People are moved by the invitation, and ultimately, they do not have to walk the aisle alone.

From my experience in white churches, we are more likely to prefer personal space during our time of worship. Eye contact or physical interaction with one's neighbor in the pew might be considered intrusive, if not downright inappropriate. The closest experience to confrontive touch that I have seen in the white church culture is the rite of *passing the peace*. This ritual may be practiced in a range of ways and with varying degrees of formality or warmth. But where I have typically experienced such a ritual time of greeting in the white church as a perfunctory moment of brief civility, the comparable ritual moment in the black church is more often a full-bodied affair!

I have come to revel in the effusive and affectionate prevalence of touch in the black church. Perhaps because that community extended its warmth and welcome to me in a time of intense isolation, I found a healing balm in the firm grip and embrace of the lean and in the personal connection of confrontive touch. Such physical expressiveness in fellowship as well as worship cements for me a feeling of connection and intimacy with my brothers and sisters in God's family.

BILL'S REFLECTION

In 2008, at an alumni meeting with 150 ministerial graduates of Bishop College, I witnessed an amazing moment—the singing of the Bishop College alma mater. I often have the opportunity to hear alma maters sung in a variety of venues, but this singing was different from any I have ever previously experienced.

With no real direction, the alumni spontaneously formed a straight line, interlocked arms, swayed back and forth, and began to sing, some crying as a shared experience flooded their souls. The power I felt in that room was phenomenal. I witnessed the demonstration of closeness, a sharing of experience, and a fellowship between people with a common allegiance.

I've experience similar feelings when visiting the homes of many African American men and women of God. I feel the same power of touch there. I am always greeted with the lean from the husband and a hug from the wife. Meals and the evening's conversation begin with holding hands and standing for grace. And at least in my experience, speaking the words while holding hands in unity, love, and respect appears to be the norm.

Recently, I had just that exact experience while dining in the home of Rev. Dr. Walter Malone Jr., pastor of Canaan Christian Church in Louisville, Kentucky. On the way home, my wife and I reflected about what we had experienced within the privacy of a meal shared by people of God—one white couple and one black couple—with the nothing but the cross of Jesus connecting us across centuries of division. It truly was the power of touch and a connection being made that left a lasting impression.

JOEL'S REFLECTION

The power of touch in some black churches may even extend to anointing the foreheads of parishioners with oil, a practice seldom seen in most expressions of white, evangelical Protestant Christianity. The oil is often applied by one of the pastors or elders in the church. While I have seen the practice many times, I cannot say that it is a widespread in the black church, but it does occur and can carry great meaning.

Rev. Dr. Ralph Douglas West Sr., pastor of the Church Without Walls in Houston, Texas, sponsors Diamonds in the Rough, a program joining mature women as mentors to younger women in an effort to help the younger participants navigate their lives. At the conclusion of the program, in front of thousands of congregants, Dr. West anoints the young women with oil with the signing of the cross. It is evident from the congregation's collective response that this unction is deeply moving and leaves an indelible impression on the young women. The tactile combination of personal contact from the church's founding pastor and the essence of oil that remains must be a moment of high spiritual formation in the lives of these young women.

The practice of anointing with oil is biblical. But white evangelical churches often fear the accusation and label of being too charismatic in the use of biblical anointing, even though the practice belongs to the most ancient forms of patristic Christianity. The combination of oil and touch in a high moment of consecration belongs to the collective memory of the faith and often demonstrates what cannot be expressed in words.

RESPONSE FROM REV. DR. RALPH DOUGLAS WEST SR.

Both Bill Crouch and Joel Gregory have adequately interpreted and comprehended both the therapy and significance of touch in the African American church experience. Physical interaction is a very real part of our heritage. These tactile acts of affection are central to the black church. The expression of physical touch as a greeting probably begins in the African American home and becomes a practice and familiar ritual we teach our children.

In relationship to the church, touching begins long before the worshipper enters the sanctuary. Often the same greeting within the church walls can be encountered in the parking lot. Within the sanctuary, before the first musical note is played to kick off worship, several people will have made their way around the room to embrace or shake hands and lean toward one another.

In each service there is almost a silent confession whispered in every pew: "I need someone to affirm me today." Most worshippers have survived the week without validation, acknowledgment, or recognition, but Sunday is the day of affirmation. Long before the phrase "turn to a neighbor" was made popular in some church services, members of African American churches turned to others with little prompting or coercion. It was and still is a natural occurrence.

So, touching is very much a part of our tradition, culture, history, and personality, as well as being a crucial part of our ministries. We are a tactile people. The Gospels indicate that Jesus came preaching, teaching, and healing. The first two can effectively be accomplished without putting hands on the hearer. Touching and healing, however, fit like a hand in a glove. Healing is absent without physical touch.

The lean, as Bill and Joel have referred to it, is actually a universal nonverbal greeting among African American men that communicates unity and brotherhood. Its use can be rather humorous. For instance, I may meet someone for the first time, but should I discover we come from the same place, that becomes reason enough to invite the sacred touch. To an outside observer, however, the gesture might mimic a secret society handshake.

On the other hand, Joel's observation about the confrontive touch bespeaks of the church serving as a community. The African American church community understands the proverb, "It takes a village to raise a child." You do not raise children without laying hands on them. Equally, the church embraces the power of touch as both a visual and tactile demonstration of what authentic Christian fellowship should look like.

RESPONSE FROM MIN. LESLIE J. BOWLING-DYER

Touch has the power to affirm life or destroy it. Through the power of touch, we can affirm or denigrate, can promote inclusion or alienation, can encourage healing or inflict injury.

Black worshipping communities have long employed life-affirming touch in active resistance to the messages of a dominant culture that has historically denigrated and abused black bodies. In the context of worship, black bodies become instruments of praise. The role played by ushers is emblematic of this consciousness and offers us an additional point of reflection on the power of touch.

Beyond their duties of regulating movement into, out of, and within the sanctuary, ushers are also tasked with aiding parishioners in times of physical need. When congregants are overwhelmed by grief or are "caught up in the Spirit[1]," ushering becomes a very tactile and intimate act. It is not uncommon in the black church to see ushers fanning a congregant or wiping the sweat and tears from someone's face. While such acts of care are not the exclusive domain of ushers (nearby congregants will often take part), ushers invariably take the lead in these activities.

I recall the poignancy of an usher's touch one Sunday as I observed her tending to a woman parishioner who had been caught up in the Spirit. In tending to this woman, the usher lifted the parishioner's hair, fanned her neck to cool her, and dabbed perspiration from her neck and brow. Once the parishioner had regained her composure, the usher departed. I was simultaneously repulsed and moved by the idea of the usher helping this woman. I recognized in the usher's actions an unconditional, loving touch that exemplifies familial intimacy. It was a scene that brought to mind the story that is told in John 13:3-20 of Jesus washing the disciples' feet.

Initially Peter rejects Jesus' offer to wash his feet. Jesus' response, "Unless I wash you, you have no share with me" (John 13:8), should not be read as purely kerygmatic in nature. Jesus' words suggest that a lack of touch can invite alienation. Jesus is seeking intimacy with Peter that can only come when the bounds of personal space and autonomy give way to caring touch offered in service.

New Testament scholar Rev. Dr. Allen Dwight Callahan, in his commentary on John's Gospel, notes that Jesus' service is rendered not as a slave to a master but as a family member to another family member. Callahan asserts:

> Foot washing is a service customarily rendered by a slave. But the Gospel of John avoids the language of slavery to describe discipleship, and Jesus explicitly rejects slavery as a metaphor. . . . Jesus is not an obedient slave; he is an obedient Son. His followers are not his slaves; they are his "little children."[2]

Ultimately, Callahan's skillful analysis draws out the distinction between one who serves as a result of coercion and alienation and one who serves as a result of familial love and inclusion.

Viewed through the lens of John 13:3-20, the loving service performed by ushers becomes a fulfillment of Jesus' call "to wash one another's feet" (John 13:14). In the context of the family of God, we are to extend to others and receive at the hands of others loving touch that affirms our familial bond as sisters and brothers in Christ. The service offered by ushers is yet another way that life-affirming touch is institutionalized and normalized amidst many black congregations.

I affirm the welcoming touch between men, such as that identified by Crouch as the lean. I do not begrudge my brothers a gender-specific expression of affirmation; however, I would caution that a broader context of mutuality is needed, otherwise this affirming touch could be experienced as exclusionary. Too often people are ascribed, both in the church and society, varying levels of worth, importance, and influence based on class, age, and gender. My enthusiasm for the lean is tempered if the congregational context in which it is being practiced does not affirm male-female partnership and mutuality at all levels of church life. The truly good intentions of the lean will be compromised if the gesture becomes aligned with practices that attribute to men, solely based on gender, greater authority and, therefore, greater worth and importance. This attribution simultaneously creates a women's sphere marked by subservience, powerlessness, and diminished worth.

What I appreciate about the service-oriented, loving touch of a diverse usher board—male and female, adults and youth, all with varied socioeconomic statuses, serving among an equally diverse congregation—is the opportunity for Christian mutuality. Christian mutuality speaks of our common worth and honors the contribution of all to the body of Christ. My prayer is that we would use the power of touch to bring every member of the body of Christ to his or her fullest potential.

❊ Takeaways

1. Hug your brothers and sisters in Christ, for it is in that moment that the power of love is expressed.

2. Capture the true power that comes from holding hands and connecting with others. Connect with the person with whom you stand or kneel when you collectively pray.

3. Learn to engage groups in responsive expression with each other. Remember that the most ancient Christians practiced the use of touch through anointing during special occasions.

NOTES

1. To be "caught up in the Spirit" is a state that engages the emotions and manifests in any number of ways in the body, including but not limited to crying, shouting, jumping up and down, or falling prostrate.

2. Allen Dwight Callahan. "John," *True to Our Native Land: An African American New Testament Commentary* (Minneapolis: Fortress Press, 2007), 202.

CHAPTER 8

THE FIRST LADY OF THE CHURCH

Since they too are also heirs of the
gracious gift of life. . . . (1 Peter 3:7)

JOEL'S REFLECTION

Rev. Dr. J. Alfred Smith Sr., the esteemed pastor emeritus of Allen Temple Baptist Church in Oakland, California, led his church for four decades. Dr. Smith has long been considered a legend in Baptist theological circles. Throughout his ministry, Dr. Smith and his beloved wife, the late JoAnna Goodwin Smith, enjoyed years of service together. His autobiography, *On the Jericho Road,*[1] tells the moving story of their romance and their partnership in the gospel ministry, from the first day they met and throughout their enduring marriage.

For decades, she was the revered first lady of the church, even when Alzheimer's disease struck her. Dr. Smith chose to be her primary caregiver, in spite of his demanding responsibilities as pastor, educator, and denominational and civic leader in the Oakland community.

Though she was suffering from dementia, Dr. Smith still brought his wife to church. She rested in his office during the first service. In her wheelchair, with ceremony and respect, Dr. Smith accompanied her into the second service. Even though she was not fully cognizant, the congregation still honored and revered her as the first lady. After service, in addition to the multiple tasks that a pastor must navigate, Dr. Smith attended to her needs, carefully picking her up and placing her in the car to take her to lunch at a bayside restaurant.

While no one knows the intricacies of another's marriage, anyone who watched his care of her had to be more than impressed. Until the day she died, she was truly the first lady of Allen Temple.

This is a most vivid example of what I have seen in black church culture. While I fully recognize that there are numerous women in the ministry who pastor and have husbands, my experience has been mainly with the wives of African American pastors. So from my vantage point, the pastor's wife is no mere appendage or an unpaid additional worker. Whether she is a visible and vocal part of ministry, or she deems her role as one behind the scenes, the preacher's wife is central to the life of the church, and she is revered as a leader in an extraordinary sense.

BILL'S REFLECTION

It is not easy being the wife of any public figure. I think it is especially difficult being a pastor's wife under any circumstance, regardless of color, black or white. These women are heroes.

I am the son of a first lady. I never heard her called that, but as the wife of the pastor, that is her title according to some traditions in the black church. My mother was one of the most caring and loving human beings I have ever known. She reached out as a rescuer to anyone who was underprivileged. For forty years, she cared for my sister, Deborah, who was ill. And she cared for anyone in our church who was sick. A faithful Sunday school teacher and a leader of vacation Bible school, she was usually in worship unless one of her children needed her more. She was a vital presence in my father's ministry. Even though she was the first lady of our family, to the congregation she was simply a remarkable individual who also was the pastor's wife.

When Rev. Richard Gaines of Lexington, Kentucky, told me to park in the first lady's parking spot at Consolidated Baptist

Church on a Sunday when I was to preach, I did not realize the honor I was receiving. Pulling up in the parking lot, it was not hard for me to spot the pastor's reserved parking place, along with the one directly beside him for his wife.

Following the pastor's instructions, I parked in the first lady's space. Before I could walk the two hundred yards to the front doors of the church, two parishioners told me I would have to move my car because I had parked in the first lady's space. They were protecting and supporting her, and we were just in the parking lot! For me, this was something decidedly different. It was then that I noticed that the first lady in the African American church was treated with a significant measure of honor, esteem, and affection, far more so than that rendered to the pastor's wife in many white churches.

JOEL'S REFLECTION

Rev. N. L. Robinson has served as pastor of Mt. Olive Baptist Church in Arlington, Texas, for forty-three years. He is now eighty-eight years old, and the city of Arlington recognizes him as a significant leader of the community. Still incredibly sharp of mind, he maintains an astonishing grasp of the church's huge facility, school system, women's shelter, and residences for the retired. His wife, Sister Pearl Robinson, has served beside him the entire time.

In every service, Sister Pearl is recognized, asked to stand, and greeted joyfully by the congregation of thousands. With her impressive hat, perfectly-coiffed hair, and impeccable attire, she has quite a presence. When she stands, she is the symbol of enduring faith across decades of witness, from the time the church met in a simple building to the erection of its impressive facilities today.

Through the examples of Sisters Smith and Robinson, I have learned about the respect most black churches reserve for the pastor's wife. Most often, she is accorded the dignity granted to someone of royal distinction. In contrast is the sometimes-utilitarian view of the pastor's wife in other cultures. Often, she is overlooked and seldom honored as one who sacrifices privacy, time, and freedom to be married to a minister, and in too many cases, she is the target of criticism for perceived flaws, failures, or failings in the role some church members attempt to define for her.

BILL'S REFLECTION

One of the roles placed upon the first lady is that of hostess. For every church function I have attended, the preacher's wife accepts that role with grace and dignity. Whether it is a dinner in the family home, an event at the church, or a banquet downtown, these women have an understanding of etiquette, the importance of image, and the significant example they demonstrate for the other women in the church.

But there is so much more.

These first ladies are smart, networked, and leaders in their own rights. Some host conferences, travel as speakers, act as business advisers to their husbands, and even serve as copastors in the church. Sheretta West, Wanda Davis, Audrey Ash, Sandra Malone, Barnetta Cosby, Carolyn Gaines, and Roszalyn Mack Akins are just a few examples of first ladies finding their places in ministry, beside their husbands and as individuals. The challenges of African American women are many, but across America, the wives of black church pastors are emerging as voices of hope and example.

RESPONSE FROM REV. JOHN K. JENKINS SR.

This chapter highlights one of the key components of a healthy church. That component—a subject near and dear to my heart— is reflected in the manner in which the pastor's wife is treated. In a black church full of healthy families and healthy people, I have rarely seen a case where the pastor's wife was treated poorly. If you find a church where the families are strong, the people are strong, and the community is impacted, you will also find a community where the pastor's wife is honored and respected.

This respect is extended to the first lady, because she is looked upon as the church's model of womanhood. She is married to one of the most important men in the community. She is the mother of his children. She is keeper of his castle. She is the one to whom he comes home after wrestling with the cares of the world.

He has counseled the hardheaded, buried the dead, prayed for the sick, fought with the know-it-alls, cried with the depressed, rejoiced with the victorious, and made all the decisions that needed to be made—all in one day! And then when he comes home to her, she makes it all well. She also has the daunting responsibility of sharing her husband's time, energy, and focus with the rest of community, and she does it to the best of her ability.

She does all this while carrying the mantle of her own calling and passions. In many cases, she pastors the women in the church in areas her husband cannot address or fully understand. Wow! She is an awesome woman and is deserving of special honor.

From the pastor, the church takes the cue in how they are to treat the pastor's wife. When he and the church recognize and acknowledge her unique and special role, not only are they honoring his wife, they are honoring all the church's women.

RESPONSE FROM DR. SHEILA M. BAILEY

In the television miniseries based on Alex Haley's *Roots,* Chicken George says, "You don't know where you are going until you know where you have been."[2] It is intriguing to reflect on the changing paradigms of pastor's wives. My parents, Deacon and Mrs. Joseph Smith, who took us as children to Faith Tabernacle Baptist Church in Stamford, Connecticut, gave me my first introduction to a 1950s pastor's wife, Mrs. Francis Baxter, wife of Dr. William Lee Baxter.

Among her responsibilities as wife, mother, choir member, and member of other organizations, I have fond memories of her working with the children and youth of our church. She didn't have a reserved seat in the sanctuary, but one was unofficially reserved for her. She taught me, as well as other girls, how to recite in public, emphasizing enunciation and poise. My mother reinforced her lessons, but Mrs. Baxter continues to be a part of who I am.

When I graduated from Stamford High School, I left Connecticut and headed south to Bishop College in Dallas, Texas. On September 15, 1965, E. K. Bailey, a handsome young man, entered the dining hall. When I saw him, I had no idea we would date for four years and become husband and wife for thirty-four years until his death. He pastored two churches during his lifetime and was founding pastor of Concord Baptist Church in Dallas, Texas. And I was with him every step of the way, as his helper and supporter—a pastor's wife.

I have known a collage of African American senior pastor's wives who have mirrored and modeled different patterns of being first ladies. From the urban to the suburban, from the local congregation to the international denominational organizations and institutions, there are first ladies whom I have observed and admired. With their diverse personalities, spiritual gifts, and remarkable talents, God has used them as "help-meets." I will refer to only a few as I consider the historical context of the first lady in the black church.

The late Dr. Weptanomah Carter, wife of Dr. Harold Carter and author of *The Black Minister's Wife as a Participant in the Redemptive Ministry of Her Husband*, said,

> That the Black minister's wife has had a great influence upon the ministerial outreach of her husband is a matter of historic record. She reiterates the historic role of being an understanding mate, a mother in the home and often a surrogate mother in the church, a leader of missions, a leader of fashions and a guide of church decorum.[3]

In Dr. Carter's book, there is an excerpt from an article written by Dr. J. Pius Barbour in 1952 entitled "Preachers and Their Wives" that describes the mindset of many preachers during that time: "The old preacher married a woman because he loved her and because he was impressed with her Christian Character and had good reasons to believe that she would love the church and its cause."[4]

It is interesting to contrast Dr. Carter's perspective with the perspective given by Mrs. Shirley Wise when she wrote *Sick and Tired of Being a Minister's Wife,* "in an attempt to tell it like it is, and not pretend that how it should be is how it is."[5] The title of that book would seem to open a different window on the experience of the church's First Lady!

Being a pastor's wife has it burdens but also has bountiful rewards, so I want to recognize some of those first ladies who preceded many of us in making sacrifices of service.[6] They have been faithful, tenacious, and compassionate role models. First, let me give kudos to just two of the mothers and spiritual mentors who have invested their time and attention in the lives of pastor's wives:

- Dr. Lois Evans, wife of Dr. Tony Evans, the first president of the Global Pastors' Wives Network, and founder of the First Lady Conference for Senior Pastors' Wives, Dallas, Texas. She provides a safe place where pastors' wives can gather and become empowered.

- Mrs. Patricia Richardson, wife of Dr. Willie Richardson, for teaching for more than thirty years the class, "The Purpose of a Pastor's Wife," for minister's wives in the vicinity of Philadelphia, Pennsylvania.

Then there are those women who have excelled academically, so that present and future generations will be equipped for the challenges of ministry:

- Tara Jenkins, EdD, wife of Dr. Charles Jenkins and a graduate of Southern Baptist Theological Seminary, Louisville, Kentucky, whose dissertation was entitled "The Identification of Essential Components for Equipping Pastors' Wives for Ministry."

- Mrs. Wanda Taylor Smith, wife of Dr. Robert Smith and a PhD candidate at The Union Institute & University, Cincinnati, Ohio, whose dissertation was entitled "The African American Woman Married to a Pastor."

The past and present leadership of the Interdenominational Ministers' Wives and Ministers' Widows Association should be recognized for their over one hundred years of leadership. I also recognize all other organizations that have provided training and support for pastors' wives. I would like to especially recognize Rev. Dr. Bryan Carter, senior pastor of Concord Baptist Church of Dallas, Texas, and his wife, Stephanie, as well as other pastors and wives who remember the widows who once served as first ladies with respect, compassion and generosity.

Now we look forward to a brighter future. Expectations are becoming more realistic as pastors and their spouses clarify and communicate their priorities as a family with each other and with the church. Couples are learning the importance of managing time, so they continue to serve each other, the church, and the community with love. Whether the African American pastoral spouse is a first lady or first gentleman, whether wearing "bling" or business attire, whether a stay-at-home parent or a corporate executive, she or he has a rich heritage and is not destined to live in a fishbowl. Pastoral spouses are increasingly free—not with selfish ambitions—but free in the Lord to soar to indescribable heights because God will give them, to paraphrase Habakkuk 3:19, feet like hinds' feet for high places.

❈ Takeaways

1. Your wife is a queen. Your husband is a king. Treat your spouse like royalty even if the church doesn't. The congregation will learn from your example and do likewise.

2. Being a pastor can be both rewarding and trying, but don't let the pains and pangs of the day push you from the one who helps you to be who you are.

3. Remember the importance of romance! Your spouse will thank you and so will your church.

NOTES

1. J. Alfred Smith and Henry Louis Williams, *On the Jericho Road: A Memoir of Racial Justice, Social Action, and Prophetic Ministry* (Downers Grove, IL: InterVarsity Press, 2004).

2. *Roots.* Screenplay adapted by William Blinn from Alex Haley, *Roots: The Saga of an American Family* (New York: Doubleday Press, 1976). Directed by Marvin J. Chomsky, et al. David L. Wolper Productions and Warner Brothers Television, 1977.

3. Weptanomah Carter, *The Black Minister's Wife as a Participant in the Redemptive Ministry of Her Husband* (Elgin, IL: The Progressive National Baptist Publishing House, 1976), 28.

4. Quoted in Carter, 28. From J. Pius Barbour, "Preachers and Their Wives," in *The National Baptist Voice,* 1952.

5. Shirley D. Wise, *Sick and Tired of Being a Minister's Wife* (Westerville, OH: Wise Works Publication, 1991).

6. Another great resource is the volume by Bishop John Bryant's First Lady, Rev. Cecelia Williams Bryant, *Letters of Light for First Ladies* (Judson Press, 2008).

CHAPTER 9

HOSPITALITY

Be hospitable to one another
without complaining. (1 Peter 4:9)

BILL'S REFLECTION

I arrived at the New Orleans airport to attend the National Missionary Baptist Convention as the guest of then-president, Rev. Dr. Stephen J. Thurston Sr. The baggage claim area was swamped with convention volunteers all wearing nametags identifying themselves as the "transportation committee." I kept asking for a seat on a van but was told that Dr. Thurston had arranged different transportation for me.

Soon, a stretch limo pulled up with a card bearing my name. The driver identified himself, put my luggage in the trunk, and asked me to get inside the car. Once inside, I positioned myself so other guests could fit in. Then the car began to move, and I realized I was alone. I was embarrassed. After stepping out of the limo at the hotel, I saw Dr. Thurston and immediately told him that I could have ridden in a van. "Oh, no," he said, "you are my guest." I truly did not understand at the time, but I do now.

Hospitality seems to be at the very core of the African American religious experience. Everywhere I have traveled in the last five years has been a lesson in the importance of hospitality and a model of how to make individuals feel special. From the way one is picked up at airports to the accommodations in the hotels to the extraordinary graciousness in the churches, there is never any doubt that one is a special guest, a brother in Christ, and a coworker in the kingdom of God.

My parents were always gracious hosts. Often guests shared our Sunday dinner table. At revival time, I remember the extra efforts my dad would make to accommodate the guest preacher. However, in my memory, it seems it was always the preacher's job to provide such hospitality. In my experience in the black church, it feels as if I am everyone's guest, and the hospitality is unequaled, from the parking lot attendant to choir members and the senior deacon.

Joel's Reflection

Rev. Ferdinand Gaines Jr. pastors First Community Antioch Baptist Church in Lutcher, Louisiana. Located astride the Mississippi River in St. John the Baptist Parish, the church has its roots in the earliest days of freedom after Emancipation and found its voice in the days of Reconstruction. Rev. Gaines has been the pastor there for thirty-five years.

When I visited the pastor and his associate ministers, they quickly learned of my love of Cajun food. One of the most famous purveyors of andouille (the tasty, lean, Cajun sausage) is Jacob's World Famous Andouille, located near the church. During my most recent trip, two of the ministers could not wait to take me by the store to buy me five pounds of sausage, and they shipped five more pounds to my home. Then they took me to our favorite Cajun restaurant, where I feasted on the bayou's beloved bounty. I was in heaven.

Every time I preach at First Community, Sister Carolyn W. Gaines, the pastor's wife, honors me with an unforgettable Louisiana down-home meal that she and other women from the church have prepared. The homemade gumbo, smothered crawfish étouffée, and Louisiana bread pudding, with all the accoutrements, have added weight to my ministry on more than one occasion. In my previous ministry experiences, it was a rare thing as an itinerant preacher to be invited to have a homemade meal and enjoy hospitality in the pastor's home—until I began to experience firsthand the hospitality offered by African American churches.

BILL'S REFLECTION

Deacon William Miller of St. John Missionary Baptist Church is a remarkable man. When I arrive in Oklahoma City, he is at the airport to pick me up. He is gracious and always makes sure my needs are met. He even helps with my luggage. We talk about our families, Georgetown College, the church, and the latest news in his city.

When we arrive at my hotel, he makes sure my luggage is immediately taken to my room. He makes certain the room is acceptable and that food has been prepared and has already been delivered. He gives me a written itinerary for my stay and then asks if I have any questions, while giving me his cell phone number. As he leaves, he announces the time of my next appointment and when he will be picking me up. Such gracious preparation and provision are the true Christian hospitality.

I have come to realize that there are many Deacon Millers within black churches—men and women with the gift and ministry of hospitality, who are committed to the church, their pastor, and their God. Now, there is hospitality in the majority white church culture, of course, but the differences are many. Guests are treated well, but hospitality is primarily a function for the staff. But in the black church, hospitality almost seems a congregational mission. If you walk through their doors, there is a collective commitment to treat you well.

For example, I was recently at a black church eating in the fellowship hall after service, and I commented on how good the tea was. Four days later, I received two gallons of the same tea shipped by FedEx by the marvelous tea maker, Mrs. Donna Jones. The gesture wasn't necessary; it was above and beyond, but it was also incredibly kind and thoughtful. And it was a gesture that will not be forgotten.

I've not inquired if African American churches provide hospitality training courses, but whether they are responsible for picking up church guests, serving as Sunday morning greeters in the parking lot, ushering during services, acting as sanctuary nurses, or just saying hello to someone they do not recognize, these individuals make an impression for the kingdom of God. Their joy is in serving the Lord, and in the process, they bring joy to God's children.

JOEL'S REFLECTION

During the summer, I serve as assistant preacher to Dr. Ralph Douglas West Sr. of The Church Without Walls in Houston, Texas, which has five back-to-back Sunday services. Sunday-morning preaching involves taking four helicopter rides between the two church locations. The challenging schedule is finished about 2 p.m., and by the time we arrive at Dr. West's home, everyone is famished.

Sister Sheretta Machell Grays West has completed the preparations for the meal she began on Saturday night. Their table is not only for the visiting preacher, but also for the young ministers and mentees, so these young people can share in a meal, fellowship, and unwind. From mid-afternoon until the shadows lengthen in their wooded neighborhood, the West's table becomes a place of mentoring, counseling, hilarity, gentle kidding, and mind-bogglingly great food.

Sister West usually serves no fewer than ten homemade dishes, offering an assortment of mouthwatering goodness, from oxtails and greens to amazing fried chicken and savory roasts, and various presentations of vegetables that are flavored with something from another dimension of seasoning. Beyond all statement, the food is good, and the conversation is inviting and just as flavorful.

I am always amazed at the hospitality extended by the West family. They are among Houston's first families and could eat anywhere they wish. Yet, they consider this Sunday meal a high point of the week. They use it to express Christian hospitality, a coming together of friends and family who can reflect on the worship and fellowship at day's end. The Wests' sons bring their friends, and those friends bring their friends. My own life has been refreshed and uplifted and the load lightened because of those memorable meals and the remarkable hospitality shown to me by a family who does not have to be so generous but is compelled to be so.

RESPONSE FROM REV. DR. MAJOR LEWIS JEMISON

Drs. Crouch and Gregory are quite correct. Hospitality is indeed at the very core of the African American religious experience. In fact, it is a central, respected, and treasured theme throughout the African American community.

Our African ancestors placed high value on the expressions of hospitality and generosity to all guests in their homes and their communities. In fact, these values are still held in many African cultures today. In those communities, the level of hospitality extended to a guest is still viewed as a measure of an individual's personal wealth and status. Hospitality is a great part of our tradition as a people.

Today we have not strayed far from our roots. In the African American community, the preparation and presentation of meals, as well as the extension of every possible courtesy to invited guests, are expressions of good home training. *Home training* is where family members young and old are taught and often reminded of a basic tenet of West-African hospitality— keep it simple, but make it delicious, cook aplenty, and offer what you have with an open hand and a loving heart.

This gift of hospitality, of course, also has a biblical basis that is encouraged in both Old and New Testament scriptures. The Law and the Prophets reinforce strongly the principle established in Leviticus 19:34, "The alien (or stranger) who resides with you shall be to you as the citizen among you; you shall love the alien as yourself, for you were aliens in the land of Egypt: I am the LORD your God." Biblical forebears were praised for their acts of kindness and hospitality, including Lot, Rahab, Ruth, Boaz, and the widow of Zarepeth. In the New Testament, in a request for a hospitable and gracious welcome for the deacon Phoebe, the apostle Paul admonished the believers in Rome: "So that you may welcome her in the Lord as is fitting for the saints, and help her in whatever she may require from you, for she has been a benefactor of many and of myself as well" (Romans 16:2). The writer of the book of Hebrews puts it like this, "Do not neglect to show hospitality to strangers, for by doing that some have entertained angels without knowing it" (Hebrews 13:2).

Knowing that kindness combined with generosity is the criteria for any wholesome Christian fellowship, those of us who are sons and daughters of the African American religious experience have been thoroughly trained and indoctrinated in a tradition passed down from one generation to the next. Hospitality in the African American tradition is not something that has been scripted or taught by any means in any class. Rather, it is lived out in practice and by example. The history of hospitality in the black church, though unstructured in many respects, is a part of the very fabric of our community which displays itself without formality or fashion.

RESPONSE FROM **REV. WANDA BOLTON-DAVIS**

I have heard it said that the person who practices hospitality entertains God himself. Perhaps it is with this attitude that the spirit of hospitality is extended within the African American church. Dr. Gregory and Dr. Crouch's experiences of receiving outstanding hospitality from their hosts is not an uncommon occurrence while visiting an African American church. Hospitality is highly valued in the black church experience, and there is intentional effort to create a welcoming environment. This is a central part of our culture and identity.

Generally speaking, pastors and church members make a point of being attentive to the needs of their guests to ensure their comfort. Whether the church is large with a wealth of resources or small with limited means, kindness and generosity are commonly and graciously offered.

As we consider the reasons for this kindness, we must first consider the time of slavery. Preachers were some of the first professionals among slaves. When blacks were discounted, discarded, and considered as outcasts, when they could not be doctors or lawyers or be deemed valuable by society, the preacher was highly esteemed among their own. African American preachers carried the Good News of the gospel, providing hope to an oppressed people.

Secondly, we can also credit the black family tradition. Historically, it has been a part of our heritage and culture to have family gatherings that center around meals and togetherness. These fellowships were often open to friends and church members. Extending hospitality to a preacher was a particular honor. Romans 12:13 and 1 Peter 4:9 were taken to heart.

I have seen this tradition throughout generations of my own family. I watched my grandmothers and my mother take pride in preparing delectable meals for their pastors. My childhood pastor, Rev. J. E. Graves, loved to come to our home to eat my mother's homemade ice cream. And she delighted in preparing it for him. My family also utilized their gift of hospitality in the church. I enjoy entertaining, but not the way my mother did. Unfortunately, with each generation, the face of hospitality in the black church tradition is changing. Home-cooked meals have diminished and are increasingly being exchanged for restaurant reservations—a sign of the times.

Although I concur with Dr. Gregory and Dr. Crouch about the warm welcome that is generally felt within the black church, I would be remiss if I did not express what I have personally experienced. Being a preacher myself who is married to a pastor, I have witnessed the unfortunate disparity in hospitality that exists within some African American churches. There are some inconsistencies in the reception I have received when I have accompanied my husband to preach and when I have been invited to preach.

While many pastors and churches have sought to be receptive and accepting of female clergy and have made many strides in this area, many differences still remain. Regardless of educational level, pastoral experience, noted accomplishments, or anointing, for the female clergy, superior hospitality is usually the exception rather than the rule.

In response to the experiences shared by Drs. Crouch and Gregory, I would say their encounters are reflective of the many black churches and pastors in the African American community. However, it is my prayer that greater consistency in hospitality is extended among all clergy, regardless of race, ethnicity, culture, or gender.

Though times have changed and generations have come and gone, it is my hope that the black church does not forget its heritage and cultural tradition of warm hospitality, not only within the church but in the community as well. I pray we continue to express an authentic kindness that historically has been a part of our culture. And let us continually be reminded of the exhortation in Hebrews 13:2.

✳ TAKEAWAYS

1. Church guests never forget the memorable attention to detail offered through hospitality. Treat your guests as you would want to be treated.

2. Opening your home and the comfort of your family table leaves an impression that can never be lost.

3. Those who receive you at airports, take you to hotels, and extend themselves throughout your trip may become some of your great friends and may enhance your ministry.

4. If you are a guest preacher, upon your return, do not forget to write a personal letter (not an email) to the pastor who invited you and to all those who extended themselves in kindness. The gesture will not be forgotten.

CHAPTER 10

GRATITUDE

Giving thanks to God the Father at all times and for everything in the name of our Lord Jesus Christ. (Ephesians 5:20)

JOEL'S REFLECTION

Dr. Robert Smith Jr. is one of the greatest preachers in all of the English-speaking world today. Dr. Smith is a preaching professor at Beeson Divinity School of Samford University in Birmingham, Alabama. He is an erudite homiletician, who teaches and practices his craft with excellence. Yet, at any conference that Dr. Smith is attending, he will be near the front row with his notebook open, taking sermon notes while others are preaching. He encourages every preacher, and he genuinely expresses gratitude for everything he hears. He is grateful to be wherever he is, be it pulpit or pew, and grateful for what he is listening to. There is a sense of gratitude about his demeanor in general.

He expresses gratitude in concrete, tangible ways. On one occasion, he approached another preacher and generously said within the earshot of others, "Here is the modern Chrysostom," referring to John Chrysostom, the golden-mouthed orator of the fourth-century Christian church. When the recipient demurred, Dr. Smith responded, "Don't take that away from me." Dr. Smith's response demonstrated a soul given to the expression of appreciation, one who considers life and the gift of ministry to be received with gratitude. He did not want to be robbed of that precious treasure.

Dr. Smith's attitude is similar to others I have encountered in black churches where I have been privileged to preach and teach. Teachings, materials, observations, and experiences that might be taken for granted elsewhere are received with unabashed gratitude that is repeatedly expressed. People with a history of oppression do not take much for granted. Life is a gift, and gifts call for gratitude expressed without dissimulation.

BILL'S REFLECTION

Rev. Dr. Melvin Von Wade Sr. is a remarkable man. He was first introduced to me when he was president of the National Missionary Baptist Convention of America. I soon discovered he also was the pastor of the Mt. Moriah Baptist Church in Los Angeles, California. There are many people who have been touched by his life and ministry, so I sensed a special quality in this man. While he has considerable influence, he is one of the humblest men I have ever met.

I was curious to know how that could be. What I've discovered is that at his core is an overwhelming sense of gratitude. As a young man, Dr. Wade was awarded a scholarship to attend Bishop College in Dallas, Texas, an opportunity that shaped his life. There, he met friends like Dr. E. K. Bailey and his wife, Dr. Sheila Bailey. Dr. Wade's ministry was launched because of mentoring faculty like Rev. Dr. Harry S. Wright, who pushed his mentees to excel academically, but also showered them with compassionate witness.

Dr. Wade's outstanding ministry was interrupted because of a life-threatening illness, a disease he has battled courageously, and one he is defeating. The joy of his life is a seven-year-old young lady he calls "Granddaughter," who is the first topic of his conversation. Every day he is grateful, he says.

Ask Dr. Wade what he is so grateful for, and he willingly replies that, first and foremost, he is grateful for his Savior, Jesus

Christ; secondly, for his family and church; and then, he begins a long litany of thanks for friends who gave him support, opportunities, and doses of forgiveness along the way. Ask what sustains him through his battle with cancer, and he expresses gratitude for all who continue to pray for him.

What I have learned on *my* journey with African American church leaders is that gratitude is at the root of their lives. I am not saying on the whole that they are perfect; no one is. What I am saying is that they recognize that their lives' miracles were beyond their own abilities to produce. They thank God, show outward thanks to friends, stand by those who stood by them with conviction, and accept new friends as a blessing from God. Those things are examples and lessons to be learned.

JOEL'S REFLECTION

A revered leader in the church and community as well as a mentor to many younger pastors is Rev. J. C. Wade Jr., who has pastored the Zion Missionary Baptist Church of East Chicago, Indiana, for forty-three years. He is part of the preaching Wade family and a brother of Rev. Dr. Melvin Von Wade of Los Angeles. Their father, the iconic Rev. J. C. Wade Sr. of Omaha, Nebraska, even has a federal post office named for him.

For several summers, I have led a seminar on preaching at Regent's Park College, the Baptist institution that is part of Oxford University in England. In 2006, Rev. Dr. J. C. Wade Jr. was the senior member of a cohort of students attending the Proclaimers Place Seminar at Oxford, sponsored by Georgetown College of Kentucky. The younger men in the seminar treated him with the deference and reverence that is often granted to senior pastors in the black community. When he spoke, he was like the old E. F. Hutton commercials, because everyone listened.

On the last day of the seminar, every preacher testified to the importance of the four days of intensive study at Oxford. Out of deference, Dr. Wade was given the final word of testimony. We were all moved by what he said. "When I started preaching," said

Dr. Wade, "some said I could never do it. Now I am studying at Oxford University." He talked of the modest beginnings of his ministry and of the personal significance of addressing those gathered at one of the world's oldest and most prestigious educational institutions. Tears flowed freely that day.

One of my most vivid memories will always be the complete lack of self-consciousness and the genuine gratitude expressed by Dr. Wade. Then-principal of Regent's Park College, Dr. Paul Fiddes, observed that the group of mostly African American preachers attending Proclaimers Place that year was the largest group of African American pastors to ever attend an educational event, not only at Regents Park, but also in his memory at Oxford University. Dr. Wade, feeling the significance of that moment, knew that walls had come down and expressed gratitude for all those who had traveled so far.

BILL'S REFLECTION

Dr. Sheila Bailey is one of the most remarkable women I know. She is bright, radiant, full of personality, and has a love for Jesus Christ that is very apparent. In 2003, she was thrown an incredible curveball when her husband passed away unexpectedly. I first met her through the book she, her husband, and her daughter wrote, entitled *Farther In and Deeper Down*,[1] a reflection on the ministry she and her children offered Dr. Bailey during his battle with cancer.

But the book could have been entitled *Gratitude*. On every page, there was a tone of thankfulness—thankfulness for nurses, a loving congregation, special moments, volunteers, prayers, and phone calls. Death stole a man in his prime, but in the midst of his dying, a family demonstrated gratitude to God and all God's children.

I now serve with Dr. Sheila Bailey on two boards. And she remains one of the most grateful people I have ever met. She thanks everyone for the littlest of things, whether it is a phone call, a connection, or the recognition of a grandchild's birth.

Whenever she speaks, she begins by expressing appreciation to those who have helped her. She credits her husband, "Bailey," for most of the successes in her life. This woman of God is making a difference in the world, and I am simply grateful God put her in my path.

So, as far as I am concerned, there is something special about the gratitude expressed by my friends of color. History has thrown them curveballs, not just the personal ones that we all experience, but ones simply because of the color of their skin. Racism is real. Resentment and anger could be so prevalent that their attitudes toward white members of the majority culture could be anything but kind. But that has not been my experience. Instead, my black friends of God demonstrate the power of forgiveness that results in a spirit of gratitude.

RESPONSE FROM **DR. MELVIN V. WADE SR.**

When Drs. Crouch and Gregory first gave me this honor and assignment, my initial thought was to be deep, heavy, and philosophical. I wanted to be linguistically accurate and to expose my erudition. From a human standpoint, when you know that something may travel around the world, there is the demagogic temptation to be impressive.

However, it dawned upon me that, if I am truly a man of gratitude, it should be known to whom I am grateful. So instead of trying to be heavy and deep, I want to be very practical and leave on record the names of the persons who have had the greatest impact on my life and on my preaching, teaching, and pastoral ministry. I remember hearing Dr. Gregory say, "Everybody knows John Wesley, but nobody knows the name Peter Bohler. Peter Bohler was the man who led John Wesley to Christ." Because of that statement by my friend, I will in these next few lines share the names of those to whom I am so grateful.

First, there is my father, my idol, my hero, Dr. J. C. Wade Sr., a man who was ahead of his time and an awesome doctrinal and evangelic preacher. My mother, Mrs. Mary Wade, constantly shared the word *power,* as it relates to my preaching. She always said, "Son, make sure that you preach with power." My other mentor is my brother, James C. Wade Jr. I am alive today because, when I was diagnosed with leukemia, he was a six-out-of-six perfect match, and he shared his marrow with me.

I thank God for Jacquie Gantt Wade, my wife of forty-one years, as of this writing. My life has been enhanced because of my two friends of more than forty years, Drs. L. A. Kessee and Dr. E. K. Bailey. My sister, Doretha, who now resides with the Lord, taught me how to sing. My college dean, Dr. R. A. Rollins, challenged me to be studious and not to waste an opportunity, and for that I am most grateful.

My adopted godfather, Dr. S. M. Wright of Dallas, Texas, and Dr. G. T. Thomas, Dr. J. S. Stewart, Dr. S. J. Gilbert, Dr. E. S. Branch, and Dr. Robert H. Wilson are all men whom God used to recommend me to the churches I have pastored. Dr. George Banks and Dr. R. A. Williams encouraged me to return to school to get my degrees of higher learning. I want history to record that these people played major roles in my life, from the start to this present time.

Let me conclude by saying that the American Bible Society's Contemporary English Version interprets Psalm 118:29 this way: "Tell the Lord how thankful you are, because he is kind and always merciful." So, I tell God, "Thank you for favor, and thank you for those whom God so sovereignly and providentially placed in my life to shape and to mold me into who I am today."

RESPONSE FROM REV. DR. BARBARA J. BOWMAN

Historically, the black church has been the one place where black folks could assemble and fully express their gratitude to God. Today, early on Sunday mornings, black folks assemble to express gratitude to acknowledge the hands of God at work in unexplainable ways. We thank God for God's help and care. Our gratitude comes from deeply rooted acknowledgment of God's protection and knowing that God has been there in the life of the black church and its people—God has guided and has provided. This gratitude is in response to God's faithfulness. Many have experienced God's presence and power that enabled and empowered them to face barriers and obstacles. Gratitude is saying thank you to God for hope in hopeless situations and for light at the end of life's long and dark tunnel. In the midst of difficult circumstances, the black church recognizes the power of expressing thanks to God, because God provided life-sustaining resources that helped the church and its people to survive.

No sweeter fragrance permeates the heavens than that of expressions of gratitude from those who have been or who are marginalized, poor, oppressed, or incarcerated. I speak of those who have been touched and transformed by the presence of the church. I have worked and ministered to those in prison, so I am well acquainted with the struggles of those who are incarcerated.

I speak of a young African American male who had been in prison but gave thanks for the church and its members for visiting him while he was behind bars. How marvelous to watch this young man give thanks that the church had cared for his family and had received him back as a brother. He was thankful for seeing Jesus in action in his life. This young man was thankful to God for the pastor and the deacons who continued to mentor him. He was grateful for the church members who showed up for his court appearances and who wrote letters to him while he was behind bars. He no longer takes life or time for granted. He has moved forward with gratitude to God for his healing and for answering his prayers, the prayers of his family, and the church community. That is gratefulness.

For the black church, the reasons for gratitude to God remain relevant in today's world and in our community. The church is grateful to God for being able to touch the lives of people in a way that says that there's power in giving thanks to God for divine intervention in mountain-and-valley circumstances. The black church remains on the battlefield for the marginalized, poor, oppressed, and incarcerated.

❋ TAKEAWAYS

1. Send handwritten notes of thanks or praise to those who make a difference in your life.

2. Publicly thank three people during every worship service.

3. The Golden Rule still applies, so teach your children and grandchildren to be grateful for one another and for the gifts God has bestowed on them.

4. Be grateful for every venue of service and every opportunity for learning and preaching the Word. Take nothing for granted.

NOTES

1. E. K. Bailey, Sheila Bailey, and Cokeisha Bailey, *Farther In and Deeper Down* (Chicago: Moody Publishers, 2005).

CHAPTER 11

EMPOWERMENT

*What is the immeasurable greatness of his
power for us who believe, according to the
working of his great power. (Ephesians 1:19)*

JOEL'S REFLECTION

Rev. Dr. Clarence E. Glover serves the Mount Bethel Baptist
Church in Fort Lauderdale, Florida. His wife, Beulah, is the
superintendent of the church's school, which serves children from
kindergarten through the fifth grade. Together the Glovers and
their congregation are renewing a section of the church's inner-
city neighborhood. Mount Bethel has a program, developed in
association with the city, to help families buy their own homes.
Through the Mount Bethel Family Resource Center, participating couples are required to attend a yearlong class on credit-
worthiness and financial management. There, they learn the skills
necessary to becoming financially savvy.

Starter homes are also being built through a related corporation where participants can acquire special mortgages and, after
one year, move to a conventional loan. The program brings a
sense of empowerment, lifting everyone involved. Young couples are able to establish credit and become homeowners. The
community around the church is gradually being renewed, with
the church becoming the center of empowerment and city leaders celebrating the outcome—a win for everyone.

This kind of empowerment reflects the holistic concerns of the black church. At its root, it is the old, old story of the gospel. Jesus hung his head and died on the cross, but early Sunday morning, he got up. When he got up, he got up with the same concerns he had in Galilee: feeding the hungry, clothing the naked, and healing the sick. It is the classic social gospel. The Jesus preached about in black churches is a holistic Jesus who cares about everything and makes the church the center.

School systems, women's shelters, job programs, credit unions, political activism, after-school tutoring, AIDS awareness, housing, and drug rehabilitation belong in the same sentence with the resurrection, atonement, and new birth. Sometimes the sacred and the secular can have common denominators.

In 1955, black churches in Montgomery, Alabama, for example, provided the spiritual succor for the epochal bus boycott. While members made sacrifices for social justice, walking to work each day for a cause, at night they gathered to gain strength, hear encouraging words from community and national leaders, and to sing about Jesus—his life, death, and resurrection. There was no separation between the quest for social justice and the journey of Christian discipleship.

Without question, in the black church, the Jesus who is worshipped is interested in spiritual birth and the coming resurrection of faithful believers. But he is a whole Jesus, not a bifurcated Savior who cared for a person's physical needs when he walked in Galilee but who now cares only for one's eternal soul. The Jesus whom my black colleagues serve is concerned for one's salvation by and by, but he also cares if one has enough to eat here and now. That is why black churchgoers can sing "We Shall Overcome,"[1] as well as "My God Is Real."[2]

I have had the privilege of conducting a number of interviews with Rev. Dr. Gardner C. Taylor. Dr. Taylor has never separated warm, Christian devotion from biting social commentary. To use the language of an earlier era, he does not separate the vertical (loving God) from the horizontal (loving neighbor).

In his sermon on Philippians 3:12-14, "A Christian Plan for Living,"[3] Dr. Taylor preaches with prophetic pointedness to the shortcomings of the American experience, putting the onus on the white community to act justly toward those it has systematically oppressed, and he challenges the black community to excel in such a way that uneven playing fields get leveled. In the sermon's next movement, Dr. Taylor addresses with Christian piety his personal desire to pray more and his keen expectation that he will see Jesus and be made like him. In black preaching at its best, social justice is always connected to the wellspring of transcendent personal piety. What God has joined together stays connected in black preaching and church life.

BILL'S REFLECTION

No matter how small or large the church, the mission of every black man or woman of God whom I have met remains consistent: They want to empower their congregations by cultivating the emotional, financial, physical, and spiritual capacities of their members.

At the First Baptist Church Bracktown in Lexington, Kentucky, I sat amazed in a Sunday service when the pastor, Rev. Dr. C. B. Akins Sr., announced to his congregation a get-rid-of-debt strategy. He spoke frankly about the crisis of personal debt, especially pertaining to credit cards. He asked several deacons, already equipped with glass jars and scissors, to come forward. Then he implored those in the congregation who were losing the financial battle to cut up their cards and deposit the remains in the jars, while offering the names of financial planners to get them on the right track. Folks streamed down the aisles.

Two Dallas, Texas, churches, St. John Church under the dynamic leadership of Rev. Denny Davis, and Friendship-West Baptist Church pastored by the prophetic and theologically gifted Rev. Dr. Frederick D. Haynes III, are two of the many churches offering to their members an entire curriculum of opportunities geared toward empowering their lives, from spiritual to physical to financial concerns. These pastors understand that resources must be made available in an effort to provide life-changing prospects for their members.

Rev. Dr. Kevin W. Cosby, pastor of St. Stephen Church in Louisville, Kentucky, has taken empowerment to a whole new level with the rebirth of Simmons College of Kentucky. Dr. Cosby is trying to educate an entire community. Founded in 1879, in the wake of the Depression, the historically black Simmons College found itself close to extinction, forced to sell its original campus and relocate to a single office building elsewhere in Louisville. When Dr. Cosby agreed to become the college's new president in 2005, he soon developed the motto, "A Rendezvous With Greatness." In 2006, the college bought its old campus with the help of Frank Bridgewater, a member of St. Stephen Church and a construction-company owner, and moved the school back into its original setting in 2007.

Quoting from the college's website, "Simmons College of Kentucky is an institution of biblical higher education dedicated to educating people in the urban context through strong academic and professional programs in order that they may become productive citizens and agents of change in society."[4] That really is true empowerment.

JOEL'S REFLECTION

Traditionally, black churches have not always been able to afford large staffs. However, with the growth of numerous black churches that have huge congregations, that situation is certainly changing today. But the black church has not always been privileged to say, "Just hire someone to do the job." So a cadre of lay leaders is often trained and developed to address issues of programming, education, and the overall concerns of the church.

The pastor empowers those leaders to do the necessary work of the church. From special events, such as church and pastor anniversaries, Men's Day, Women's Day, and music programs, to bigger tasks like long-term strategic planning and development, hospice ministries, and youth-related concerns, tasks are often led by volunteer leadership. Lay leaders are entrusted with large areas of church life. This creates a system that grows leadership from the inside and fosters a sense of commitment from those who carry out the tasks.

This system also empowers church members to serve. For example, for many people, the usher board represents a position of pride and authority. These devoted members do not merely hand out bulletins and guide worshippers to preferred seats. They are empowered to help conduct the service, provide some security, assist during the offering, and help with the widest range of needs. At the national conventions of black Baptists, there are special breakout meetings for ushers from across the nation. This gives the individual church usher a sense of solidarity with the church universal. I have developed the highest regard for these servants who stand at the door of the Lord's house.

The transportation ministry is another humble but significant ministry where leadership qualities of otherwise average individuals have the opportunity to shine. While on the face of it, this ministry may seem mundane, as a traveling preacher I know firsthand of its importance. As I observed in a previous chapter, the laypeople who execute this ministry do so with precision akin to that of a drill team. They do not fulfill their duty as a tiresome task but as a personal assignment and one of significance. I witness this ministry's skill and care week after week, and I continue to be impressed.

Similar praise could be offered to those who serve in other, more visible or traditional leadership roles—the deacons, the associate ministers, the Sunday school superintendent and Christian educators. These are simple examples, but they have made indelible impressions on my ministry.

BILL'S REFLECTION

My first visit to the Eastern Star Church in Indianapolis, Indiana, with Rev. Dr. Jeffrey Johnson Sr., was full of surprises. I was amazed to learn the breadth of the church's ministries in its numerous church locations in the city. Dr. Johnson prepares carefully to ensure that each ministry is effectively done at each planting. As a college president, I was especially intrigued by his Jewel Christian Academy, a private school that serves children from kindergarten through the fifth grade. As I spoke with the teachers, I observed wonderfully disciplined classrooms and learning at its best taking place.

Dr. Johnson, like many other black pastors across the country, believes that education is the key to the true empowerment in his community. In these private academies, a foundation of discipline and strength is provided for children that will carry them through the challenges they will face. Empowerment, however, is not only for the children. Dr. Johnson and others understand that many of the adults in their congregations need empowerment as well.

So Eastern Star Church also initiated the Jewel Bible Institute, which is an adult education program designed to empower its members to gain a deeper understanding of the Word of God. The Jewel Bible Institute may eventually partner with Georgetown College, enabling their adult education program to be online so more members can have the opportunity to utilize it as an empowerment tool.

For three years, I served as a vice president of Carson Newman College in Jefferson City, Tennessee. Only five miles from my office was the small town of New Market. Hundreds of times in my tenure there, I drove through the town on my way to Knoxville. Little did I know that New Market was the home of the Highlander Research and Education Center, the place where, for seventy-five years, African American leaders, including Dr. Martin Luther King Jr., have been trained in social justice activism. The center's mission is to work with people struggling against oppression. The first black speaker at a workshop arrived in 1934, and by 1942 the center's activities became fully integrated. In 1953, Highlander changed its focus from labor concerns to the civil rights movement. If you go to their website today, you can find a picture of Dr. King, folk singer and activist Pete Seeger, Rosa Parks, Charis Horton (daughter of Highlander cofounder

Myles Horton), and Rev. Dr. Ralph D. Abernathy standing in front of the Highlander library.

Today, the Highlander Center focuses its efforts on other social issues and people who need advocates in society—including groups across the South and Appalachia, as well as immigrant populations. On campus in front of the Center stands a sign declaring, "We [hope] we can encourage people struggling for justice in their communities, while at the same time building connections across race, ethnicity, nationality, gender, sexual preference, class, and age that will lay the groundwork for a broad movement for social and economic justice."

This is just one of the many places where black ministers and laypeople have trained to empower others. How could I, a Baptist minister who was working just five miles away, not know about this amazing empowerment facility? How did I miss it and the opportunities that could have been born?

Dear God, continue to open my eyes that I may see.

RESPONSE FROM REV. DR. GINA M. STEWART

Bill and Joel conclude correctly that empowerment is important in and to the black church.

In the summer of 2009, I, along with several other African American pastors, was invited to attend a luncheon hosted by the Billy Graham Evangelistic Association (BGEA), to explore the possibility of hosting a Rock the River tour. The Rock the River tour is an evangelistic summer concert for youth, featuring top Christian rock and hip-hop bands. The one-day outdoor event travels up the Mississippi River from Louisiana to Minnesota, packed with seven hours of high-voltage music and brief, challenging messages by Rev. Franklin Graham. The Rock the River tour is Franklin Graham's response to his burden to reach a lost generation of young people with a message of hope.

The representatives from BGEA envisioned a partnership between black and white as well as urban and suburban pastors and churches. This was a lofty goal, considering the racial polarization that characterizes the city of Memphis, Tennessee.

As we engaged in an open and transparent discussion about the opportunities and challenges of such a venture, one of the pastors stated that if the tour came to Memphis, his participation would be contingent upon an economic benefit being guaranteed to African American vendors and service providers. In this pastor's opinion, this was a reasonable expectation considering that the predominant population in Memphis is African American.

This statement led to a discussion of the importance of liberation theology and empowerment (specifically economic empowerment) to the African American experience. As the representatives from BGEA listened intently to our perspective as African American pastors, Rev. Dr. Eugene L. Gibson Jr. of Olivet Fellowship Baptist Church made the observation that on the slave ships, slaves and slave masters worshipped two different Gods. The slave master worshipped the redeeming God, while the slaves worshipped the liberating God.

Gibson's comments suggest that the priority issues of importance for black churches tend to differ from those of majority culture churches. The black church has historically advocated for social, political, and economic empowerment. The black church, out of necessity, has had to minister to the whole person. As Dr. J. Deotis Roberts states in his book *The Prophethood of Black Believers,*

> The Black church has been sensitive to social justice issues from its inception because it has been ministering to an oppressed people. Therefore, interpretation of the gospel of Jesus Christ in the Black church tradition has been concerned about justice as well as love. Justice and love cannot be separated.[5]

The black church has had to minister to the whole person because it rarely had the luxury of separating individual salvation from collective salvation. Consequently, the black church has typically focused on a much broader agenda, by addressing issues related to racism, poverty, economics, civil rights, and injustice, as well as issues of personal piety, holiness, ethics, and righteousness.

As C. Eric Lincoln and Lawrence H. Mamiya state in the book, *The Black Church in the African American Experience,* "The notion has persisted that if God calls you to discipleship, God calls you to freedom."[6] History has wrought subjugation and oppression to African Americans and, as a result, certain institutions were formed in order to aid African Americans spiritually, economically, and culturally. The African American church has served as one such anchor institution. From its inception, the black church has provided many social services such as teaching slaves how to read and write, providing health and burial insurance to church members, encouraging and facilitating voter registration, and establishing schools and colleges. Many contemporary black churches continue this tradition of not just ministering to the soul but also providing for concrete, everyday needs.

An ethic of empowerment as espoused by the black church rejects a privatized faith, which places an emphasis upon a highly spiritualized notion of salvation to the exclusion of a political understanding of salvation. Orthopraxy is just as important as orthodoxy (see James 2:20-22). Faith that is geared toward a private praxis with no consideration toward the elimination and eradication of dehumanizing political and social structures reveals that the deeper concerns of humanity are not necessarily priorities.

As Dr. James Cone states in the preface of his book *God of the Oppressed,* any analysis of the gospel that did not begin and end with God's liberation of the oppressed was ipso facto unchristian.[7] When personal faith refuses to incorporate a political understanding of salvation, sin is no longer private and personal, but social and public. The gospel of Jesus Christ is one which assures God's people that God is concerned for their entire well-being as central to the divine will.

Although empowerment finds meaningful application in politics, economics, and social relations, it is also valued as a highly spiritual transaction that both invokes and responds to the divine presence as mediated through moral agency and human interaction. As an African American female pastor, I must say that empowerment must not only be practiced, it must be preached as well. As a product of a denomination where certain Scripture passages have often been used to oppress and exclude women, to enforce domination rather than strengthen, affirm, and fortify, I can personally attest to the importance of preaching empowerment.

The role of women in the black church has always been critical to its survival. Historically, African American women have comprised the majority of membership, have contributed a large percentage of its financial support, and have played a unique role in the nontraditional leadership and power of the black church and the civil rights movement. Despite their numerous contributions and sacrifices, women have often been the ones who have felt the sting of the triplets of racism, classism, and sexism, not to mention the deafening silence on the issue of domestic violence.

I am indebted to my pastor and predecessor, Rev. Eddie L. Currie, and others like him, such as the late Rev. Shirley Prince, Dr. Cynthia L. Hale, Dr. Renita Weems, Dr. Elaine Flake, Dr. Jacqueline Grant, Dr. Carolyn Knight, Dr. Floyd Flake, Dr. Jeremiah A. Wright, Dr. Fred C. Lofton, Dr. Edward Parker, and Dr. David Larry Boyle, for their commitment and courage to practice *and* preach empowerment. When we preach empowerment, we invite the critique of all forms of oppression and disenfranchisement. When this happens, we bring the realities of our existence to the preaching moment and place them under the reign of God.

RESPONSE FROM REV. DR. JOSEPH EVANS

Dr. Crouch understands African American churches and their role to empower people holistically. There is a reason for that role historically. Newly emancipated African Americans established three things after slavery: houses of worship, houses of

education, and burial spaces for their dead. These were socioeconomic and sociopolitical statements introduced to the larger
majority. Before the visible institution, these three things were
preexisting traits that belonged to the invisible institution. Worship, education, and entrepreneurship are the center of African
American life. The only other entities that compare to the black
church in significance to their communities are the New Testament Jewish synagogue and the African communal systems.

Passages such as Luke 2:25-40 and Acts 3:1-10 are examples
of a biblical Jewish worldview that was holistic, not individual-
istic. Synagogues function best when their communities are con-
ditioned to survive, strive, and thrive. Bill Crouch's observations
on black churches are similar to New Testament descriptions of
Jewish synagogues, when he says the mission of every black man
and woman of God he knows is to empower their congregations
by cultivating the emotional, spiritual, and financial capacities of
their members.

Similarly, I think the black church identifies with an African
communal worldview. The legendary preacher Rev. Dr. Wyatt
Tee Walker affirms this when he writes in his book *Afrocentrism
and Christian Faith,* "The profit economy is a western idea;
nothing in the history of African peoples is suggestive or akin to
individual gain. All of the structures and dynamics of West
African life have to do with an economy that is shared by all
according to need."[8]

Dr. Walker's definition is of a communal economy, not a
Marxist or communist socioeconomic order, but an African
sense of holistic participation. Dr. Gregory reveals his understanding of this participation and correctly writes, ". . . empowerment reflects the holistic concerns of the black church," and,
"The Jesus preached about in black churches is a holistic Jesus
who cares about everything and makes the church the center."

What Drs. Crouch and Gregory have observed is a holistic
approach to life, which is very New Testament Jewish, old-world
African, and African American in its point of departure.

RESPONSE FROM REV. BERNESTINE SMITH

I am in agreement with Drs. Gregory, Crouch, and Evans' comments on empowerment. However, I would like to expand the discussion. The black church, as I know it, has been faithful in empowering laypersons for a servant ministry in the local church and in community ministries. These ministries are designed to communicate God's love through words and deeds. They indicate that Christian living is not just talk, but a walk. They prove true the words of James that faith without works is dead.

In empowering laypersons young and old to become participants in holistic ministries—meeting people's mental, moral, physical, and spiritual needs—many church members discover new lifestyles of service and the fulfillment gained from Christian service.

But when it comes to empowerment in the black church, there are some areas of weakness, such as the division in our faith over the role of women in ministry. There are still churches that will not license or ordain female pastors. Some even hesitate to welcome women as deacons. As an educated woman minister, ordained in 2000 and assigned to seniors ministry, I have found full acceptance in our church from the seniors and their families and from the larger community.

I am called upon to preach the gospel, to baptize, to serve the Lord's Supper, to officiate at funerals, and to conduct special services on the liturgical church calendar. I provide counseling and pastoral care, and I supervise female and male student ministers from the theological seminaries of the Oakland-San Francisco Bay area who are seeking fieldwork and credit. Other ordained women clergy serve with me on the Allen Temple pastoral team, led by our senior pastor, Dr. J. Alfred Smith Jr. But such support and acceptance is not the case for all women who seek this path.

Not enough is being done to empower women to respond to God's call upon their lives. The fear of empowering women, especially those seeking the ministry, stunts the spiritual growth of the church and rejects the mandate of Ephesians 4:11-12, which calls all believers to use their gifts to edify the body of Christ.

Dr. Smith has fostered an environment at Allen Temple where women feel empowered. Many are in positions of influence; for example, Rev. Dr. Malvina Stephens serves as the minister of congregational care and as director of the prison ministry; Rev. Dr. Eunice Shaw is director of social service ministries; and Rev. Brenda Guess, a candidate for a doctorate in education, is dean of the leadership institute. Rev. Patricia Gardner and Rev. Brenda Douglas serve along with Dr. Harold Orr in supervising at least twenty ministers-in-training, most of whom are women. Room for women has been made at the ministry table, and Dr. Smith has helped to make that a reality.

When women leave staff positions at Allen Temple to serve as senior pastors elsewhere, it has been necessary for them to serve Presbyterian, Methodist, or United Church of Christ congregations, which openly welcome women pastors without reservations.

Young adult women who are working in executive and corporate levels in secular America are hurt when churches are unwilling to empower them to serve in all areas of church leadership. This practice of excluding women is contrary to Galatians 3:28, which says: "There is no longer Jew or Greek, there is no longer slave or free, there is no longer male and female; for all of you are one in Christ Jesus."

❊ TAKEAWAYS

1. Consider the importance of social justice ministry and how it shapes and impacts the church.

2. Invite your community's black ministers and leadership to break bread, and offer to partner with them to empower a neighborhood, a school, or even your congregation. Combine resources; great things could happen.

3. Join with black churches in your area to do a community project, and then consider a joint worship experience. Blessings will abound for everyone.

NOTES

1. "We Shall Overcome" is the title of a traditional civil rights protest song, which many believe was derived from the refrain of "I'll Overcome Someday," hymn written by Charles Albert Tindley (1901).

2. "My God Is Real" is the title of more than one gospel song, the best known of which is perhaps the one written by Kenneth Morris.

3. Gardner C. Taylor, "A Christian Plan for Living," in *Great Preachers*, Series 1. The Odyssey Charmed Collection, VHS, Gateway Films, Worcester, PA, 1997.

4. http://www.simmonscollegeky.edu/documents/46.html (accessed February 19, 2010).

5. J. Deotis Roberts, *The Prophethood of Black Believers* (Louisville: Westminster John Knox Press, 1994), 90.

6. C. Eric Lincoln and Lawrence H. Mamiya, *The Black Church in the African American Experience* (Durham, NC: Duke University Press, 1990), 4.

7. James H. Cone, *God of the Oppressed* (Maryknoll, NY: Orbis Books, 1997), xix.

8. Wyatt Tee Walker, *Afrocentrism and Christian Faith* (New York: Martin Luther King Fellows Press, 1993), 6.

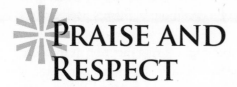

CHAPTER 12

PRAISE AND RESPECT

Outdo one another in showing honor.
(Romans 12:10)

JOEL'S REFLECTION

Dr. Eric A. Johnson is pastor of Greater Galilee Church in the inner city of Louisville, Kentucky. On this particular Sunday morning, children of all ages, from very young children to high school students, were asked to gather around the pulpit. They were invited to face the congregation because they had achieved success in school—from rewards for exemplary behavior to exceptional honor-roll grades. The pastor called the names and then personally congratulated each student. Individual achievement became a community and congregational experience, with multiple generations joining the celebration.

This community celebration reflects at least two aspects of African American church life—its integration of both individual and communal experience and its synthesis of sacred and secular life. Historically and traditionally, the African American church has served as the center of African American life, so individual and personal achievement becomes a community victory, leaving little division between the secular and the sacred. Aspects of life that I have not seen being routinely celebrated in white majority culture churches are often occasions for rejoicing in black churches. It is the way a community affirms itself and its young people.

An exceptional report card might earn a mention at the family dinner table in some cultures, but it is a matter for a standing ovation and collective praise in most African American churches. The African American church members desire to make sure their children's accomplishments are celebrated, because that may be the only setting in which their work is recognized. It is here that the division between secular life outside the church and spiritual life inside the church merge, and what happens in one's everyday existence can be cause for recognition on Sunday morning.

But there is probably a subtler undertone to the celebration as well. Historically, the dominant culture has often required from blacks double the effort; African Americans must be twice as good at whatever they embark upon in order to be equal. Established prejudices, lowered expectations, and outright lack of assistance make the achievements of African American high school honor graduates something worthy of celebrating. Education for African Americans has been a key to freedom, so a good report card is more than praiseworthy.

BILL'S REFLECTION

It took me a while to recognize that there was a distinct pattern of praise and respect punctuating most gatherings in the African American church, whether during Sunday morning worship or at an afternoon gospel choir concert. From my experience, every meeting, lecture, and sermon begins in almost the same manner, with a litany of those in attendance who hold positions of importance, members who have done something exceptional that week, or people who have somehow positively interacted with the speaker. They are recognized, and their names are called from the pulpit in an act of homage, and to be honest, common courtesy.

As I have listened to lectures at the E. K. Bailey International Expository Preaching Conference, have attended the four national black Baptist conventions, and have worshipped in African American churches across the country, I have been awed by the praise and respect these pastors have shown to each other, to important visitors, and to faithful parishioners, before any other order of business has commenced. For example, a sermon may typically begin this way: "To Rev. Dr. Julius R. Scruggs, president of the esteemed National Baptist Convention, USA, to the deacons, to the elders, and to the brothers and sisters of the historic White Rock Baptist Church, it is my honor and joy to be with you on this day."

The visiting pastor may acknowledge the deacon who provided transportation during his or her stay, or the minister might mention the couple who provided fellowship and dinner on a particular night during the revival. The point is simply that public respect, praise, and recognition are regularly given.

And, I must admit the practice truly surprised me. It is markedly different from what I have traditionally experienced throughout most of my ministry. I am sure there are a variety of reasons why African American pastors take the time to recognize one another, but recognition is clearly an indication that the speaker arrived at that particular event and time, not by himself or herself, but because of a list of individuals who, by position or relationship, have made an impact. Those who have offered their assistance are thanked for that reason.

As a man of God, I know the impact of certain people on my life, and I try to express my gratitude to those special people occasionally but I almost always do so privately. However, I am learning from black men and woman of God that a public expression of praise and respect is very, very powerful and has a lasting impact.

JOEL'S REFLECTION

In many arenas of the white religious community and majority culture, referring to people by titles of position is falling out of use over the last few decades. The trend is toward decreasing formality in address and interaction. I remember clearly in the

1980s how surprised I was when I heard a noted minister, Rev. Dr. Charles R. Swindoll, then senior pastor of First Evangelical Free Church in Fullerton, California, being addressed by everybody inside and outside his church as Chuck. My sons grew up going to Chuck E. Cheese's restaurants, and I associated the name *Chuck* with the children's entertainment venue—not with a famed preacher. The informality felt disrespectful toward a leader of such distinction and age.

In the Baptist churches of my boyhood, the deacons and the pastor were at least addressed with the fraternal title *Brother*. If that practice has not completely vanished, it has at least diminished to a rarity in what I have experienced in white churches. I know of a minister who pastors a large, predominantly white church and who holds a PhD from a prestigious seminary, but who is called by his first name in and out of the pulpit by church staff and *even* by young children.

Yes, I know. Shedding our titles was supposed to make preachers and pastors more accessible and human, touchable and more informal. Yet, something has been lost in translation over time. I cannot name it, define it, or identify it, but something has been lost and remains missing.

In contrast, titles and positions in the black church are acknowledged and used almost without exception. There is much history behind this. Pastors and their spouses are usually not addressed solely by their first names. The pastor may be referred to as Reverend, Pastor, or more casually, Doc. The pastor's wife, the first lady, may be addressed as Mrs. Smith or Sister Smith. If a first name is used, it is coupled with an honorific. For example, the first lady may be referred to as Sister Cynthia or Mrs. Jan. The minister would be Pastor Chris or Rev. Casey. Finally, pastors who have been at their churches for a long time may have acquired an affectionate but appropriate nickname, but traditionally they are not called solely by their first names, except by those very close to them.

Years ago, when I first started preaching in black churches, and with ears dulled by the growing first-name familiarity of my white Baptist background, I immediately noticed the ubiquitous use of titles connoting academic achievement and position. Black brothers and sisters used the titles naturally, without pretense and with the real intention to acknowledge position and achievement.

While this tradition has particular historical significance, the habit does lend a sense of dignity and gravity to the pulpit and to the general social concourse of the churches. In the hallways, in the pulpit, at the table, and in the home, a sense of respect appears to permeate the lives of those intricately involved in the black church.

There are deep cultural reasons for this, I know. Among the many indignities forced upon blacks when Jim Crow reigned was the pervasive use of first names only when whites addressed blacks. So an eighty-year-old black man was addressed by his surname, or even worse, was called "Boy." A culture so historically and systematically demeaned should and does have every reason to treasure the well-earned titles of achievement, for they were hard fought.

The implications of showing respect by referring to people by their professional titles or the use of honorifics are numerous and profound. Among other things, it may mean that the pastor of a black church may not be treated merely as a hired hand. For many in African American society, a pastor is a figure of weight and substance, both in the church and in the community.

Some white pastors I know lament their marginalization and demotion and often feel like hired functionaries. In fact, some say they are not even considered first among equals with the laity in their churches. But the remedy is actually simple: give people the respect they are due, because old-fashioned manners have modern-day import. We can start the process by not letting sixth-grade children refer to elders by their first names. Respect.

BILL'S REFLECTION

The Mighty Men of Valor Conference, headed by Rev. Dr. Clifford Ashe III, senior pastor of DaySpring Ministries in Middletown, Pennsylvania, is a remarkable experience. The music and devotional worship led by Rev. Frank Wilson certainly gets everyone in the praising mood. Within minutes, all two thousand men are on their feet, singing and praising God in an extraordinary way. On the last morning of the conference that I attended, when Rev. Ashe was being introduced, the audience was asked to stand and honor their leader. The roof shook with applause as Rev. Ashe came to the podium.

While visiting the historic Abyssinian Baptist Church in Harlem, New York City, I was struck by Rev. Dr. Calvin Butts III's adept ability to acknowledge so many people for their work within the church and community. He was eloquent in his praise, but he was equally careful to be very personal. Dr. Butts wanted to take the necessary time to let his congregation know he was grateful for their efforts and work for the kingdom of God. Those who were mentioned glowed from their pastor's recognition. It was incredibly effective and genuine.

Rev. Dr. Russell Awkard, pastor of the New Zion Baptist Church in Louisville, Kentucky, and a moderator of the General Association of Baptists in Kentucky, is masterful in how he praises others. I have heard him on several occasions bring up an individual's name and speak about his or her accomplishments in glowing terms. Black church pastors appear to have a remarkable ability to express gratefulness and to say thank you in a public manner that creates a sense of pride and enhances their ministries. When I have the opportunity now, I try to do likewise.

RESPONSE FROM REV. DR. VALERIE MILES-TRIBBLE

Many African American adults can readily recall their childhood introductions to public speaking and singing, as well as their roles of responsibility, from acolyte to junior deacon, from youth usher to worship leader on their special Sunday. These introductions to leadership were pivotal but traditional and expected experiences in the black church. Sunday school and holiday programs provided oratory roles, and today's youth find additional creative expression in liturgical dance troupes, or as participants in rites-of-passage rituals.

As Joel reflected, the communal celebratory praise and recognition tendered by pastor and congregation toward these youth are the mustard seeds that can grow with the nurtured development of their self-esteem, and will remain part of these students' life-changing memories. Just as a youth's self-worth may flourish, an adult's can also be enriched.

Wise is the pastor in any church who also remembers to recognize and affirm his or her adult congregants for their service and sacrificial work. In church, as well as in business settings, when people feel affirmed and respected, there is an increased commitment to the work at hand. In fact, Bill reflected on the patterns of praise and respect he witnessed in protocols that are deeply ceremonial—those that recognize position and location in public speaking forums. From my womanist theological lens that is attuned prophetically to the marginalized fringes of our society, I also raise a caution for pastoral leaders on the equitable use of praise and respect.

The human tendency is to remember selected individuals with frequency—the influential board member, the well-respected deacon, larger tithers, public figures, or more famous members of the congregation: judges, doctors, professional athletes, entertainers, or lawyers. Too often this occurs at the risk of forgetting the daily efforts of ordinary people who love the Lord and serve their church. The larger the congregation, the less likely the pastor is able to know everyone, but in any church, individual needs for praise and respect exist.

This expectation and need is essentially linked within the historical black church as the true sanctuary, where our elder ancestors—otherwise forced to tolerate the indignities of inequality and substatus as societal citizens—could exercise their minds, hearts, and voices in roles and relationships dignifying their personhood. Part of that dynamic was an expectation to be addressed appropriately, for the varied reasons Joel aptly noted in his second reflection.

In a society that tends to foster generational informality, our church tries a both-and approach that stems from yet another cultural tradition that Joel mentioned: a sense of the church as a faith family. To balance the formality of using titles such as *Mr.* and *Mrs.,* we encourage youth to understand the church family as their extended village. So, it is not unusual to hear young people address adults with relational respect, using titles such as *aunt* or *uncle,* rather than using the adult's first name.

The practice resonates in the proximity and recognition of respect existent among family for their elders, rather than a derogatory connotation in meaning, if used for subjugation between adults.

Of course, patterns or practices that are contextually conducive in one black church congregation may differ in another, but the overarching thread is to foster respect between generations and peers. Unfortunately, the nuanced practice of praise and respect is disparate among pastoral leaders and congregations where gender inequity is still at issue at local and denominational levels.

Publicly, pastors need also to be aware of the subconscious message conveyed to congregation and peers with the dichotomous use of titles in situations where female clergy leaders are present. In a time when numbers of male clergy firmly resist collegial recognition of females, a practice still occurs of respectfully referencing fellow males as Doc, Reverend, Pastor, or Esteemed Bishop, while reference in the same setting is differentiated toward the female counterpart as Sister or worse, by use of her first name, to psychologically dismiss the equity and respect of the role that appropriate use of her clergy title would convey.

This dichotomy is quickly observed and copied by the congregation, making it harder for female clergy in the black church setting to gain the respectful aura of positional acceptance that her academic or vocational achievements would otherwise command.

A consciousness-raising assessment of equity issues is found in the seminal book by now-Bishop Vashti McKenzie, *Not Without a Struggle.*[1] But gender challenges to praise and respect are not limited to the black church, as discussed by Sarah Sentilles in her book, *A Church of Her Own: What Happens When a Woman Takes the Pulpit.*[2] I think Joel and Bill have captured much of the practices and values of praise and respect that are integral to undergirding the black church experience. Nevertheless, nuances of the practice also can undermine elements of praise and respect, if they are not equitably fostered. Men, women, youth, and the seasoned adult can thrive with experiences of mutually shared praise and respect.

RESPONSE FROM **REV. STEPHEN J. THURSTON SR.**

The church's role in the African American community has been, is, and will always be pivotal. Whatever happens at home, at school, on the job, at the grocery store, at the gas station, or at the mall during the week comes together on Sunday morning to be celebrated or made right by the praise-and-worship period, the singing of the choir, but most assuredly by the preaching of the gospel. It is how we express the who, what, and why we are as a people.

Many people in the congregation have had similar experiences during the week, and so, coming together as one on a Sunday morning can create a sense of unity. Academic, social, and political achievements must be celebrated with the brothers and sisters at the church. It is the perfect setting for an attentive, captive, and sensitive audience to explode with pride for those who have done well, and to give spiritual support to those who are struggling. It is about communing with family. The church is family in the African American tradition, and the public affirmation and applause is priceless.

Traditionally, the African American church has been the place of acceptance and respect. For example, the school janitor who may suffer several indignities during the workweek may also be a faithful deacon who is in charge of helping those who come to the church in need of assistance. That position gives him or her a sense of belonging and pride.

The midweek worship service or prayer meeting makes it possible for believers to come together before Sunday morning, and allows many members who are unable to participate on Sunday to worship with their church family. Midweek services also give ministerial staff and others an opportunity to give leadership at this time. By so doing, family members and friends are able to share in a very personal and affirming way with those who are in charge of the worship.

The African American church gave birth to leadership in our communities. It provided teachers, was the first line of defense during the civil rights era, and so much more. When the larger community shut African Americans out, the church gave us hope, healed our wounds, and made us stand up and declare that there were better days ahead. That was, is, and will always be Good News!

❀ Takeaways

1. Every Sunday, publicly praise those who have made a difference in your church or in your life. Your affirmation of others will encourage everyone. More ministry volunteers may even step forward!

2. Throughout your week, in staff meetings, personal conversations, or ministry encounters, regularly thank those who have made an impact on you, from the deacons and Sunday school teachers to committee chairs and church secretary.

3. When you are a visiting speaker, acknowledge the hospitality and generosity of those who have invited and hosted you. Do it publicly, and your praise will bless them.

4. Consider the return of titles and respect for ordination, academic achievement, and position. If you act worthy of respect, that respect may come back to you tenfold.

Notes

1. Vashti McKenzie, *Not Without a Struggle: Leadership Development for African American Women in Ministry* (Cleveland: Pilgrim Press, 1996).

2. Sarah Sentilles, *A Church of Her Own: What Happens When a Woman Takes the Pulpit* (Orlando: Harcourt Books, 2008).

AFTERWORD

I love the black church.

I love her rhythms, movements, and cadences. I love the sway-ing choir director and the sonorous sounds of her larger-than-life preachers. I love her traditions and liturgy and the call and response of a faithful and engaged congregation. I love her music, from ancient anthems and African-ancestored work songs to contemporary gospel music. I love the anticipation of the Word. I love the wide hats and broad shoulders. I love her commitment to the least and to the lost. I love the feeling of acceptance when one enters her doors. And I love the hand that holds mine when prayers are lifted in praise.

I love the black church.

I am not a minister, a theologian, or even a seminary student. I am just a Pacific Northwest-born-and-bred preacher's kid, a fourth-generation American Baptist gone United Church of Christ, who spent a lifetime in the presence of some of this nation's most gifted African American pastors. I was the girl in the room when my Papa and Wyatt Tee Walker would talk about issues of social justice and would debate the "Negro Question," and who was awakened in the middle of the night because "Uncle Jesse" (as in Jesse L. Jackson Sr.) or Leon Sulli-van was standing in the kitchen wanting a hug. Now I work, write, and volunteer for pastors across the country.

I know that doesn't give me any true theological currency, but it does give me an incredible sensitivity and respect for the calling of ministry. So, after reading and editing Drs. Gregory and Crouch's book, my sensitivity gauge indicated with blessed assurance that these two white men of God have an abiding affection for that which I hold most dear.

I must admit, when first brought onto this project, I was skeptical. I just wasn't sure how these two credentialed white theologians could dissect and evaluate the black church, an institution that has fed and nurtured so many souls but is not innately and intimately a part of who they are. The black church does not seep through their pores as it does those born to it. One can never know fully another's experience. So, I wondered out loud, "How in the world are they going to pull this off?"

Well, I think they did. In *What We Love about the Black Church*, the authors simply talk about *their* experiences from *their* vantage points and allow a number of black pastors from across the country to dialogue in print about their conclusions concerning black worship and how white congregants can learn from the black church's example. Drs. Crouch and Gregory are not presenting themselves as scholarly authorities on the black church, but merely as blessed recipients of her grace and her goodness.

In an effort to bridge gaps of understanding around the most segregated (but not segregating) time of the week, Sunday morning, Drs. Crouch and Gregory opened themselves for comments and courageously welcomed what was said in response. They wrote about what they had observed and had experienced in black worship and about the distinct differences between black culture and their culture. For them, the African American worship experience is connected and tactile, personal and holistic. So they dialogue about twelve aspects of the church, including the power of touch, laughter in the midst of pain, free expression, preaching, mentoring, and encouragement, and they share what they believe sets the black church apart from the majority white church.

Because the black church is not monolithic, the responses from the African American ministers show some disparity. There is wide agreement with the authors, but also variation in nuanced shades of gray. But the common denominator from all the pastors about our church and our faith, the tie that binds all the responses, is rooted in our historical narrative—the story of our people who were brought to a land against our will. *That narrative cannot be learned or even duplicated.*

Almost every response references the fact that the modern-day black church was shaped by the legacy of five hundred years of oppression. That kind of history will not be shed lightly. So Sunday-morning worship is a time of release and praise, prayer and thanksgiving, because the God of our weary years, the one who brought us to this place at this time, has never left us alone. The nineteenth-century hymn writer Ludie D. Pickett said it best:

> I've seen the lightning flashing; I've heard the thunder roll.
> I've felt sin's breakers dashing, which almost conquered my soul.
> I've heard the voice of my Savior, bidding me still to fight on.
> He promised never to leave me, never to leave me alone![1]

That, to me, *is* the essence of the black church.

Drs. Crouch and Gregory should be commended for building a bridge that may actually lead to a destination. If one heart can be changed, if there can be greater understanding about who we are as a people, our faith and our way of worship, then their efforts will not have been in vain. Another hymn writer had something to say about that as well!

With Hope,
Rhoda McKinney-Jones
Editor
Communications Director, Samuel DeWitt
Proctor Conference, Inc.

NOTES

1. Ludie D. Pickett, "Never Alone," arr. Fred Jackey, 1897 (Public domain).

ABOUT THE CONTRIBUTORS

Sheila M. Bailey is president of Sheila Bailey Ministries in Desoto, Texas, and respected widow of the late Rev. Dr. E. K. Bailey. A popular Bible teacher and consultant, she received an honorary Doctor of Humanities from Dallas Baptist University. Dr. Bailey also serves as trustee for Georgetown College in Kentucky and for LeTournear University in Texas.

Wanda Bolton-Davis is executive director of Victorious Disciples Ministries, Inc., in Cedar Hill, Texas. With extensive previous experience in the area of adoption and women's ministry, Rev. Bolton-Davis now serves as minister of discipleship and teaching pastor at St. John Baptist Church in Grand Prairie, Texas, where her husband, Denny D. Davis, is senior pastor.

Leslie J. Bowling-Dyer served with InterVarsity Christian Fellowship for 14 years. A recent graduate of American Baptist Seminary of the West, she now serves as minister at Allen Temple Baptist Church in Oakland, California, where she lives with her husband and son.

Barbara J. Bowman, DMin, is deeply involved with community outreach ministries, including previous service as youth pastor at Allen Temple Baptist Church, Oakland, California, and work with the prison ministry at First Baptist Church North in Indianapolis, Indiana. She earned a Doctor of Ministry from United Theological Seminary in Dayton, Ohio.

Bryan L. Carter succeeded the late E. K. Bailey as senior pastor at Concord Missionary Baptist Church in Dallas, Texas, in 2003. In addition to other community and denominational roles, Rev. Carter serves as vice president of the board of E. K. Bailey Ministries and as director of membership for the African American Pastors Coalition of Dallas.

Jini Kilgore currently serves as assistant to the pastor at HighWay Ministries in Los Angeles, California. An adjunct professor of English composition at California State University, Dominguez Hills, Rev. Kilgore is also pursuing a Doctor of Ministry at Haggard Graduate School of Theology at Azusa Pacific University.

Denny D. Davis is senior pastor of the 10,000-plus-member St. John Church, with congregations in Grand Prairie and Southlake, Texas. In addition to his pastoral role, Rev. Davis also serves the Missionary Baptist General Convention of Texas in a variety of capacities.

Joseph Evans, PhD, is senior pastor of Mount Carmel Baptist Church in Washington, DC. Dr. Evans also teaches preaching at Wesley Theological Seminary and at the Divinity School at Howard University.

Cynthia L. Hale, DMin, is senior pastor of Ray of Hope Christian Church (Disciples of Christ) in Decatur, Georgia, cochair of the Samuel Dewitt Proctor Conference, and necrologist for the Hampton Ministers' Conference, among other roles. With an earned doctorate from United Theological Seminary in Dayton, Ohio, Rev. Dr. Hale is author of *I'm a Piece of Work: Sisters Shaped by God* (Judson Press, 2010).

Ivan Douglas Hicks, PhD, is senior pastor of the historic First Baptist Church North in Indianapolis, Indiana. Having earned his doctorate in African American studies at Temple University in Philadelphia, Pennsylvania, Rev. Dr. Hicks recently accepted the office of associate dean for a new African American studies department at United Theological Seminary in Dayton, Ohio.

Donald Hilliard Jr. is senior pastor of Cathedral International Church in Perth Amboy, New Jersey. He is presiding bishop and founder of the Covenant Ecumenical Fellowship and Cathedral Assemblies, Inc., and author of six books, including *Church Growth from an African American Perspective* (Judson Press, 2006).

Major Lewis Jemison, DMin, is pastor of St. John Missionary Baptist Church in Oklahoma City, Oklahoma, and a past president of the Progressive National Baptist Convention. His organizational affiliations include the NAACP, the Urban League, and National Council of Churches, as well as Georgetown College (Kentucky) and Langston University (Oklahoma).

John K. Jenkins Sr. is pastor of First Baptist Church of Glenarden in Landover, Maryland, a member congregation of Converge Worldwide (Baptist General Conference). Rev. Jenkins, who holds an honorary doctorate from Southern California School of Ministry, is a trustee of Bethel University in St. Paul, Minnesota.

Jewel M. London, DD, is founder of SOW Ministries in Houston, Texas, an organization formed to cultivate the Souls of Women. A popular teacher and preacher in her city and region, Dr. London is a member of St. Stephen's Baptist Church, where she is deeply involved with prison ministry.

Valerie Miles-Tribble, DMin, is associate pastor at Imani Community Church in Oakland, California. Rev. Dr. Miles-Tribble is adjunct professor at both the San Francisco Theological Seminary and American Baptist Seminary of the West, while also pursuing a PhD through Walden University in Minneapolis, Minnesota.

A. Louis Patterson Jr. is pastor of the Mount Corinth Missionary Baptist Church in Houston, Texas. As a renowned preacher, revivalist, and lecturer, Rev. Dr. Patterson has spoken at the Billy Graham Evangelistic Crusade, the E. K. Bailey Expository Preaching Conference, the Hampton Ministers' Conference, and National Baptist Convention gatherings, among many others.

Pamela R. Rivera is pastor of St. Luke AME Church in Waco, Texas, and president of Women in Ministry for the Tenth Episcopal District of the African Methodist Episcopal Church. Rev. Rivera is currently pursing a Master of Divinity at Truett Theological Seminary, also in Waco, Texas.

Bernestine Smith serves at Allen Temple Baptist Church in Oakland, California, as pastor to seniors in the Allen Temple Arms ministry. As a bivocational minister, Rev. Smith also works full time as a senior account manager at Kaiser Permanente.

Susan K. Williams Smith, DMin, is senior pastor of Advent United Church of Christ in Columbus, Ohio, as well as a trustee of the Samuel DeWitt Proctor Conference. Her book *Crazy Faith: Ordinary People, Extraordinary Lives* (Judson Press, 2009) was a finalist in the 2009 National Best Books Awards.

Gina M. Stewart, DMin, is pastor of Christ Missionary Baptist Church in Memphis, Tennessee. With an earned doctorate from Interdenominational Theological Seminary in Atlanta, Georgia, Rev. Dr. Stewart serves as trustee for the Samuel DeWitt Proctor Conference and as member of *The African American Pulpit*'s advisory board.

Al B. Sutton Jr., DMin, is senior pastor of the Sixth Avenue Baptist Church in Birmingham, Alabama. Recognized as a leader in the Birmingham community, Rev. Dr. Sutton earned the Doctor of Ministry from Virginia Union School of Theology in Richmond, Virginia. His doctoral concentration was in Cross Cultural Education with an African American emphasis.

Jacqueline A. Thompson is assistant pastor at Allen Temple Baptist Church in Oakland, California. Nationally recognized by BET and *The African American Pulpit* as a rising young leader, Rev. Thompson is currently pursuing a doctorate at Fuller Theological Seminary in Pasadena, California.

Stephen J. Thurston Sr. is copastor of New Covenant Missionary Baptist Church in Chicago, Illinois. Rev. Thurston also serves as project director for Canterbury Affordable Housing in Atlanta, Georgia, as CEO of the Kaptlst Korporation, and as national youth ministries director of Rainbow PUSH Coalition.

Melvin V. Wade Sr., DMin, is pastor of the Mount Moriah Baptist Church in Los Angeles, California. A past president of the National Missionary Baptist Convention of America, Rev. Dr. Wade has served his denomination in many capacities, including on the board of the National Council of Churches.

Maurice Watson, DMin, is senior pastor of Beulahland Bible Baptist Church in Macon, Georgia. In addition to other honorary degrees, Rev. Dr. Watson earned the Doctor of Ministry from Beeson Divinity School in Birmingham, Alabama.

Ralph Douglas West Sr., DMin, is the founding pastor of The Church Without Walls in Houston, Texas, and president of Ralph Douglas West Ministries. With an earned doctorate from Beeson Divinity School in Birmingham, Alabama, Rev. Dr. West has been inducted into the Martin Luther King Jr. Board of Preachers of Morehouse College.

What We Love about the Black Church celebrates what's unique about the black church while at the same time offering a bridge for understanding, appreciating, and reconciling.

For a more academic view of reconciliation and diversity, we encourage you to seek out these books by Curtiss Paul DeYoung:

Coming Together in the 21st Century: The Bible's Message in an Age of Diversity
Curtiss Paul DeYoung;
Foreword by Cain Hope Felder

"Curtiss DeYoung has worked tirelessly to bring the issue of racial reconciliation and racial justice to the attention of the Christian community. In this new edition of *Coming Together*, DeYoung reminds us that the journey towards biblically-based diversity is a difficult one, but one worth traveling. He has pulled together his personal reflections as well as additional essential voices in this dialogue to provide a thoughtful, biblical, and needed challenge for the church."

—Soong-Chan Rah, author of *The Next Evangelicalism* and Milton B. Engebretson Associate Professor of Church Growth and Evangelism, North Park Theological Seminary

This newly revised and expanded 15th-anniversary edition offers readers an in-depth study of multiculturalism and diversity in Scripture. With nearly 50 percent new material, *Coming Together in the 21st Century* features contributions from ethnically and culturally diverse men and women who offer their unique perspectives.

978-0-8170-1564-0 $19.00

800-458-3766
www.judsonpress.com

JUDSON PRESS
PUBLISHERS SINCE 1824

Also by Curtiss DeYoung

Reconciliation: Our Greatest Challenge— Our Only Hope
Curtiss Paul DeYoung

"Curtiss DeYoung deftly takes up the burning question of the church's potential leadership role in race relations and reminds us that meaningful change will cost something. *Reconciliation* is a provocative but highly readable work about daring to make strangers and enemies begin to view one another as friends and equal members of the body of Christ."

—Cain Hope Felder, Howard University

"In *Reconciliation* Curtiss DeYoung offers us a moral guide and practical road map through this difficult, painful, and ultimately liberating process called reconciliation. This is a book that should be read by every American who wants to build bridges across our great divides—which should be all of us."

—Jim Wallis, Editor-in-Chief, *Sojourners*

978-0-8170-1256-4 $15.00

Beyond Rhetoric: Reconciliation as a Way of Life
Samuel George Hines and Curtiss Paul DeYoung

The late Samuel Hines, who was African American, and Curtiss DeYoung, who is Caucasian, provide an inspiring, practical theology of reconciliation that will enable readers to take concrete action.

978-0-8170-1329-5 $10.00

800-458-3766
www.judsonpress.com

JUDSON PRESS
PUBLISHERS SINCE 1824